IKIGAI

Achieving Happiness & Harmony With Yourself And With Others, Guiding By The Ancient Japanese Philosophy

Clarissa Mona

Copyright © 2022 Clarissa Mona All rights reserved.

No part of this guide may be reproduced in any form without permission in writing from the publisher except in the case of brief quotations embodied in critical chapters or reviews.

Legal & Disclaimer

The information contained in this book and its contents is not designed to replace or take the place of any form of medical or professional advice; and is not meant to replace the need for independent medical, financial, legal or other professional advice or services, as may be required. The content and information in this book have been provided for educational and entertainment purposes only.

The content and information contained in this book has been compiled from sources deemed reliable, and it is accurate to the best of the Author's knowledge, information and belief. However, the Author cannot guarantee its accuracy and validity and cannot be held liable for any errors and/or omissions. Further, changes are periodically made to this book as and when needed. Where appropriate and/or necessary, you must consult a professional (including but not limited to your doctor, attorney, financial advisor or such other professional advisor) before using any of the suggested remedies, techniques, or information in this book.

Upon using the contents and information contained in this book, you agree to hold harmless the Author from and against any damages, costs, and expenses, including any legal fees potentially resulting from the application of any of the information provided by this book. This disclaimer applies to any loss, damages or injury caused by the use and application, whether directly or indirectly, of any advice or information presented, whether for breach of contract, tort, negligence, personal injury, criminal intent, or under any other cause of action.

You agree to accept all risks of using the information presented inside this book.

You agree that by continuing to read this book, where appropriate and/or necessary, you shall consult a professional (including but not limited to your doctor, attorney, or financial advisor or such other advisor as needed) before using any of the suggested remedies, techniques, or information in this book.

TABLE OF CONTENTS

INTRODUCTION

"Ikigai" is a Japanese term that cannot be translated, but since "Iki" means "existence" and "gai" is used to indicate "purpose", we can say that it means "the purpose of life".

What is your motivation when you get up in the morning? Why do you do what you do every single day? How are you making the most of your time on this Earth?

These are those uncomfortable questions that in the West we try to avoid carefully, by anesthetizing the brain, but which in Japan (a country of great contrasts: every year thousands of people commit suicide but there is the percentage highest of happy centenarians) are part of the everyday life of most people.

For the Japanese, for example, retirement is depressing when understood as a period of life in which nothing is done. For them, every single day must be dedicated to doing something, to give a purpose to their life. In fact, a day in which nothing is done is a wasted day, which is why the Japanese do physical activity up to an apparently absurd age and always find a way to occupy their time with something concrete.

Leaving aside the different mentality, I find that the concept of Ikigai very fascinating and useful, especially for us Westerners, often tormented by existential doubts to which we cannot find answers. One above all: what is the purpose of my life?

Once they were reflections for the few, because most of the population lived to work and ended the day too tired to think about it. Today, however, the situation is quite different: in the Western world most people have the time, the education, the possibilities and the tools to think about the meaning of life.

So, many begin to wonder if their purpose is to work every day from Monday to Friday for eight hours in a detestable and demeaning activity. Or spend your entire life in the same place doing the same things, on autopilot, consuming time.

These are difficult but necessary reflections to start building a happy life. First you need to figure out if what you are doing is right for you and for your emotional well-being. If not, you need to change and move in another direction.

The problem is that a lot of people get stuck on the first step: they know they are unhappy but they don't know what they should do to change the situation. They don't know their Ikigai, their reason for being.

A person s should stand firm on his positions, should open himself to the new and not be afraid of the unknown. Also, be an explorer of the city you live in: try new jobs, hang out with new people, read new books. Do something new every day, go to places you've never been! Test yourself in many different contexts, because only in this way will you understand which one is right for you, what makes you happy and what you are capable of doing. Only in this way will you find your Ikigai. On the other hand, how do you know which door opens to the key you have in your hand if you don't try them, I don't mean all of them, but at least some? See, the world is full of people trying to crack the lock, but maybe the door is simply the wrong one! The world is full of opportunities of all kinds: explore them.

THE 4 POINTS OF THE IKIGAI METHOD

Besides being a fascinating and sobering concept, Ikigai is also a practical way to understand what your life purpose is. It is in fact the intersection of 4 elements:

- What you love to do
- What you're good at
- What can bring positive change to the world
- What you can make a living with.

Find a path that meets each of these four parameters and you will find your purpose in life. Over time, especially while traveling, I realized that my "Ikigai" is just what I previously considered one of my reasons for maximum personal fulfillment: writing.

In fact, for me writing is:

- What I love to do;

- One of the best things I can do;
- The tool to spread a positive message through the pages of this blog and my book;
- My work.

Writing is my "Ikigai", my purpose in life, what makes me get out of bed every day with a great desire to live. Thinking about my case specifically, I also found another interesting definition of Ikigai: it is what you would do regardless of everything else.

If I won €100 million in the lottery tomorrow, you can rest assured that I would continue to write anyway. Because writing is for me a passion, a vocation, a purpose, at the same time a means and an end. To use a fascinating and exotic word: Ikigai.

FIND YOUR IKIGAI AND YOU WILL FIND YOUR HAPPINESS

Obviously each of us has our own Ikigai, which is found by intersecting those four areas mentioned above. If for me it's writing, for other people it's something completely different.

For example, I know a girl who lives by the sea. Take her away from the sea and she will be miserable. Specifically, her Ikigai is diving: it is what she likes, it is what she knows how to do, it allows her to promote sustainable maritime tourism and to clean up the seas in which she dives (positive effect on the world) and finally it is her work (she has a diving school).

You can find Ikigai by becoming a teacher if you love being with children / teenagers, you are an excellent educator, you want to raise individuals aware that one day they will help the next generation and finally you get paid to carry out this profession. You can find your Ikigai in any field of life and only you can find it: there are no recipes or manuals, you will discover it through a little introspection and time dedicated to yourself.

If you want to find the purpose of your life, your reason for existing, find a common point between what you love, what you do well, what the world needs and what you could get paid for. I assure you: just like it happened to me, so you will find the coordinates of your happiness.

In this book you will find how to find out what your Ikigai is and all the secrets of the Okinawans. Because on this island its inhabitants who follow Ikigai and other precepts of Japanese philosophy have one of the highest longevity rates in the world

CHAPTER 1
WHAT IS IKIGAI?

IKIGAI is a Japanese term that can be literally translated as purpose, reason for living, or as what drives us to get up in the morning and fight. It is a method, a Japanese philosophy that has been in use for centuries and is also useful for career guidance.

IKIGAI is the name of a Japanese philosophy in use for centuries by a country that has proved to be the longest-lived in the world.

In practice, it is the ability to find a balance in the activities that fill our life in a path of self-reflection and awareness.

The aim is personal and professional fulfillment in the balance between the personal and social dimensions.

Is IKIGAI also useful in terms of professional and career guidance?

Personally, I find it very useful in the context of career guidance and perhaps to support the search for an ideal occupation for a happy and active life.

The ideal occupation is the one that crosses the 4 areas of which IKIGAI is composed:

- What I like to do,
- What I know how to do,
- What the world of work is looking for,
- What they pay me or might pay me for.

How to outline your own IKIGAI

IKIGAI is precisely the ideal area of equilibrium, strictly personal, in which the 4 aspects intersect and therefore the questions to be asked in a self-assessment process.

Two questions are personal - inward:

- What do you like to do, both at work and in your free time?
- What can you do and what skills do you have?

Two other questions are social - outward:

- What is the world of work looking for in terms of skills and competence?
- What activities or skills could they remunerate or pay you for?

It must be borne in mind that, for each person, the boundaries between the various areas are in continuous movement over time and that perhaps one could start from answering the questions relating to one's childhood and adolescence, and then come to define the current areas.

In addition, it would also be stimulating to periodically review one's vision of IKIGAI, because the vicissitudes of life, interests and many other variables could have led to deviations in the areas.

How to start the search for your IKIGAI

You can start by trying to answer the self-assessment questions also because it is essentially an intimate and personal journey.Finding your IKIGAI isn't easy, it's like a treasure hunt where the treasure is different from person to person. It depends on various factors, such as one's expectations, one's environment. Furthermore, it is constantly evolving and depends on one's personal history, vicissitudes and personal encounters.

This is not an easy path .

Ikigai (生 き 甲 斐) is a Japanese word with multiple meanings: iki means life, existence, while gai stands for purpose, reason. The translation of this term could be "something to live for" or "raison d'etre", but this is limiting.

In the Japanese archipelago of Okinawa - an area famous for the healthy longevity of its inhabitants - the concept of Ikigai means "reason to get up in the morning", so this term is often also associated with a loved one.

The search for one's meaning in life and one's vocation requires profound introspection: in fact, according to Japanese culture, everyone has an Ikigai even if they are not yet aware of it.

Let's find out together how to reveal and cultivate your Ikigai, so as to reach a state of satisfaction, happiness and awareness.

Even if Marc Winn 's diagram, taken as a reference, does not necessarily provide a precise and unequivocal answer on the meaning of life, it can be very useful for approaching the discovery of one's raison d'etre. In fact, by completing the diagram petal by petal - starting from the external ones - you can pause to reflect on your true passions, on the profession of your dreams, on your deepest vocation and on your greatest passion. In this way you will realize that mainly it is only one thing that gives depth and meaning to your existence, that makes you feel happy and motivated: this is your Ikigai.

For some the concept of Ikigai coincides with their work, for others with a particular hobby while for still others the reason for getting up in the morning is the relationship with a loved one.

Do you want to find out which is your Ikigai too? Here are some tips for a first approach to this difficult concept.

If you still don't know exactly what your personal reason for getting up in the morning is, keep an eye on the Winn diagram and follow these steps that will help you unravel your Ikigai:

Ask yourself questions: What are my passions? What do I like to do? What am I good at? How can these aspects translate into a profession? What is my mission in life? How can I be useful to others?

The only way to find your Ikigai is to dig inside yourself, ask yourself many questions and try to give sincere and unconditional answers.

Finding the answers: if the answers to these questions do not overlap but, on the contrary, are different from each other, do not be discouraged: finding a balance - reconciling passions, vocations, mission and profession - is certainly not easy. Only when you manage to harmonize all these aspects will you have found your true Ikigai and will you be able to start living more serenely and consciously.

Make a list: writing a list of everything we like to do and everything we do well can be a good exercise in getting closer to your Ikigai. The first step consists in comparing the two lists and identifying the common activities, after which we must ask ourselves how these activities can be related to the needs of other people and finally evaluate if there are related earning opportunities.

Think back to the day when you found the right match for you, the right clothes, the right accessories. You certainly felt stronger, able to overcome difficulties. On the contrary, there are days when nothing works: the dress is wrong, too long / short / narrow / wide…, the accessories are wrong. In short, you are uncomfortable and you feel more fragile. Try asking yourself: what do I want to become? What is the aspect of my personality that I want to reveal? The answers to these questions will help you get to know yourself better and can give you clues to align the image with your personality and discover your unique style.

Despite the usefulness of these exercises - to pursue the aim of knowing one's raison d'etre - life is unpredictable and cannot be built at a table. It is only by starting to act that we can unveil our Ikigai, perhaps even in something we had never thought of before.

Always dedicate yourself to what you like, and cultivate your hobbies, your passions, accept your aspects, even the darkest ones: in the end the road may not be the right one, but you will certainly not regret the path you have taken and you can feel more and more close to the unveiling of the mysterious Ikigai.

Self-acceptance is a difficult step, we are often led to criticize and "mistreat ourselves". I invite you to do a little challenge, that is: the day of kindness. I'll explain how to do it. For 24 hours you will have to be kind to yourself, respecting these rules:

Don't be offended, not even by thoughts. If your internal dialogue starts to think something unpleasant about you, stop it right away by replacing it with something kind.

If you can't stop in time and think something negative about yourself, act as if you are another person and, apologize to yourself!

Write down the feelings in the notebook, also writing which are the most difficult passages and why they were difficult.

This challenge, easy but not simple, will allow you to understand the importance of continuing to be kind to yourself and the well-being that this brings you.

When you get up in the morning, do you ask yourself what is the point of what you are doing and cannot find an answer? Do you feel that what you do, even if you do it well, doesn't bring you a real sense of fulfillment? Are you looking for something that will make you truly happy and satisfied with your contribution to the world, but you don't know how to find it?

Ikigai is all this and something more, it is the feeling of living a meaningful existence. According to the Japanese, Ikigai is the secret to a long and happy life, it is the purpose for which we get up in the morning.

According to research carried out between the nineties and the early 2000s, blue zones have been identified: demographic and geographical areas of the world where life expectancy is significantly higher than the world average. One of these is Sardinia, the other is Okinawa, the island of the centenarians. Among the various aspects that unite these centers of centenarians, in addition to a spare diet, a dynamic life and an active social life, there is a strong purpose in life felt by every inhabitant.

Ikigai doesn't have to be a "big" thing. Your family, a dream, your own work as an artisan, the care of your garden or your animals, anything can represent your Ikigai.

Sometimes, we feel that we are not in the right "place", but we don't know why, or which one is really right for us. Sometimes, we keep our dreams tightly closed in a drawer and slowly the dust and junk hide them. Sometimes, we make wishes, while we blow out candles or see a shooting star, but without really taking action to make them come true, because there are other more "important things to do".

The good news is that each of us has our own Ikigai, you just need to know where to look.

The Ikigai is the connection point between:

- The things you do well,
- The things you like to do,
- The things the world needs,
- The things someone might pay you for.

By combining passion, mission, vocation and profession in one center, Ikigai will allow you to create your own action plan to create the life you want.

What is the drive that animates you every day, leading you to do things to the best of your ability and deriving joy and satisfaction from them?

CHAPTER 2

THE 5 PILLARS OF IKIGAI

People with a lot of Ikigai live more satisfactorily, and, according to some studies, they also tend to be healthier and age better. But how do you find and grow your own Ikigai?

When I was little I liked going to school. I remember very well that sense of positive expectation with which I woke up every morning. I also remember once I started crying because I had a fever and had to miss a day of school.

That pleasant feeling, of joy and light excitement in going to meet my day, I have not experienced very often in recent years; perhaps only in special circumstances, such as holidays.

For a few weeks, however, things have changed for me. I quit my office job, and I am now curating my blog, writing my books, keeping up with social media and everything else, and it is becoming my main occupation.

Before, it often happened to me that I wished the day would end. I was waiting for the moment when I could calm down with a book or some TV series and then go to bed.

Now, however, the night before falling asleep I think: wow, I can't wait for tomorrow morning. Then maybe, in the morning, I always wake up wrong, but I feel that urge again, that desire to go towards my day. And it's wonderful.

This is Ikigai. The reason we wake up every morning, what gives our life meaning and makes us feel the joy of being alive.

Dan Buettner, an American researcher of the National Geographic Society, has long studied the habits of the Okinawans trying to understand what the secrets of such an enviable state of health can be.

It is no surprise that nutrition plays a decisive role. The diet of the Japanese of Okinawa is very rich in vegetables, they consume a lot of tofu (a kind of cheese derived from soy) and follow a healthy diet that seems to date back to Confucius. It is called hara hachi bu: a saying they recite before eating and that reminds them to get up from the table when they feel 80% full. And they have also adopted some customs that help them not to overeat, such as smaller plates and the habit of not bringing all the cooked food to the table so that each person has to get up to go and fill their own plate.

These are healthy eating habits, from which we can certainly draw inspiration too. According to Dan Buettner and other scholars, however, there are also social and psychological factors that favor the good health of the inhabitants of these islands.

Meanwhile, in their culture there is no rigid boundary between working life and retirement. In fact, Dan Buettner explains, they don't even have a word for retirement. There people remain active and continue to do their jobs even in extreme old age.

There is also a strong, connected social fabric. Okinawans often organize themselves into small friendly groups called Moai, made up of six people who support and help each other throughout their lives. I don't know about you, but I would pay to be able to stay inside one of these Moai.

But the thing that has most caught the attention of scholars - and which has since spread to the point of almost becoming a fashion - is this concept of Ikigai.

Ikigai is the meaning of life, or even why you wake up every morning, or what it is worth living for. And those with a lot of Ikigai, it seems, tend to have better health.

In a study conducted by the University of Sendai, Japan, Ikigai is defined as follows:

The sense of Ikigai does not simply reflect individual psychological factors (well-being, hope), but also the individual awareness of the motivations for which one lives; its meaning has to do with having a purpose or reason to live.

The term Ikigai is commonly used in Japan in phrases such as "this hobby is what is worth living for (Ikigai)", or "raising my children makes my life worth living (Ikigai)". In the most authoritative Japanese dictionary Ikigai is defined as feeling the joy and the sense of well-being, of being alive, realizing the value of being alive.

In short, it seems that the joy of living protects us from certain diseases and helps us to live longer. Interesting, isn't it?

Grow your own Ikigai

Ken Mogi is a Japanese scholar who works in Sony's computer science laboratory. His research fields concern the functioning of the mind and brain. He recently wrote a book dedicated to the theme of Ikigai: The little book of Ikigai. The Japanese way to happiness.

It is not a booklet to find your Ikigai. Reading it, Ikigai does not seem to be something that is found, rather something that, at best, is revealed, or cultivated.

To get closer to our Ikigai, says Ken Mogi, we can start by asking ourselves some simple questions:

- What are the things that have the greatest value to me?
- What activities do I get the most pleasure from ?
- How do I like to use the wee hours of the morning after I wake up?

This idea of Ikigai is not simply 'find your passion and follow it'. Rather, it is a personal research path, which has a lot to do with what we decide to do in our life, and with how we do it.

Doing things carefully, well, with love and attention to detail; this, according to Ken Mogi, is part of Ikigai.

It is not said that Ikigai has anything to do with success. Getting social recognition for what we do is certainly important, but our joie de vivre does not depend on this. When we carry out some activity that makes us try Ikigai, in fact, we are driven by an internal motivation, we feel pleasure in carrying out the activity itself, and not so much in the reward that - perhaps - awaits us. The idea of Ikigai approaches that of flow: that state of total immersion in what we are doing that makes us forget everything else. When we do not perceive the passage of time, and our mind, instead of hopping restlessly here and there, is focused in the present.

Sometimes in life we work with the wrong priorities and too often we do something just in exchange for a reward; if the rewards don't arrive in time, we are disappointed and lose interest in what we do. Here, this is just the wrong approach. Between actions and rewards there is almost always a certain time lag, and not even after we have worked objectively well do we have immediate recognition: reception and recognition take place in a stochastic way, based on many variables that are beyond our control. If we can make effort the primary source of our happiness, then we will have won the biggest existential challenge. In other words, keep playing even if no one is listening to you. You draw when no one is looking at you. Write a story that no one will read. The joys and inner satisfactions will be more than enough to keep you going. If you succeed in this undertaking you will become masters in the art of being in the here and now.

Here lies the meaning of life: in what makes us feel the fullness of the present, which makes every moment precious, and which gives us the feeling of having a purpose (which is something other than a simple goal to be achieved).

Our Ikigai can reveal itself in different activities, depending on what we like, which has value for us, which makes us feel alive. It can be a hobby, family care, our job, our morning run, a golf lesson, yoga, or doing volunteer work.

The five pillars of Ikigai

Ikigai rests on these five pillars:

- Start small
- Forget about oneself
- Harmony and sustainability
- The joy of little things
- Stay in the here and now

I would translate them like this.

Whatever you plan to do, start small, take small steps, and do things right.

Do not act only for the rewards, but try to put your self aside and experience the pleasure of being in the flow.

Search for harmony and sustainability, keep in mind that your actions have an impact on the world around you and on other people.

Pay attention to the little things, a ray of sunshine that warms, a cup of coffee in the morning, a hot shower after a run - these are often the things that make us feel happy and in harmony with ourselves.

Learn to stay in the here and now, try to root yourself in your present: accept it as it is and then try to improve it, if you wish (taking the first small steps, in fact).

You may have seen the Ikigai represented in a four-circle diagram.

The Ikigai diagram was elaborated by Marc Winn in a blog post in 2014. What Marc Winn did was put together the idea of Ikigai (as explained by Dan Buettner), with the Venn diagram used to represent the concept of life purpose.

This idea by Marc Winn has nevertheless been very successful and that diagram has been disseminated, modified, and reused so many times that now many assume that it represents the concept of Ikigai, but if you show it to a Japanese, he would most likely remain perplexed. The two concepts, that of Ikigai and purpose in life are not the same.

Having said that, it can undoubtedly be a very useful tool, for example for those who have not yet understood what their path can be, for those who already have a career but would like to change, or even for those who simply want to give a new direction to their life.

It is useful because it helps us to distinguish two elements: what we like to do and what we are capable of doing well. For example,

I like to listen to music and sing over it. But I'm out of tune like a cracked bell.

So it's something I do from time to time when I'm alone in the house, but I've certainly not made it an important activity in my life. I prefer to invest in writing, which I also like and certainly do a little better. If, on the other hand, I had felt inclined to sing, I could have taken lessons and participated in a choir.

The next steps are about the impact that what we choose to do has on the outside. What does the world need? It is not that in order to answer this question we must think of solving the problems that afflict humanity. Just think more simply of how our actions can affect and involve other people. Taking my passion for writing and putting it in this book goes in this direction, for example. Making cakes for the school party, for someone who loves to cook, still goes in this direction. Or even organize a reading group in the library or a club to do knitting with friends.

Asking what the world needs, and acting accordingly, means matching our passions and skills with what's out there. Without this meeting, what we want to do and achieve in life risks remaining unrealistic.

We can therefore certainly use this diagram to reason about ourselves, about our qualities, and about the direction we want to give to our life.

It is an exercise that we can also do at our desk. We can first make the list of things we like to do, then the list of things that are good for us, and see which activities are common to these two lists. And then ask ourselves if and how these activities can meet the needs of other people (first step) and if and how we can manage to get paid for it (second step).

However, there is nothing clear and definite about all this. It is an exercise that can be useful but then, to really understand something, you have to start taking action.

Let's say that the diagram of the Ikigai can help us decide what to do, in which direction to direct our efforts. The five pillars of Ikigai can tell us how to do it, with what attitude, with what intention.

And then it is only in doing, that eventually our Ikigai will be able to reveal itself. Maybe even in something that had never even entered our head. Fortunately, life is not built around the table.

CHAPTER 3
EXERCISES TO ACHIEVE IKIGAI

Ikigai is the method of finding out what's worth getting up for in the morning, making you feel like you lead a full life and be happier.

The inhabitants of Okinawa Island, also called 'the island of the centenarians', are well aware of this. In fact, on this island there is a very high percentage of inhabitants over the age of 80, in excellent health.

In this happy island you live following the rhythms of nature. The inhabitants have healthy eating habits and engage in physical movement and cultivate a sense of belonging to the community. And last but not least, they are well aware of their Ikigai.

We all have our Ikigai even if we don't always know it consciously. In order for your Ikigai to truly satisfy you, it must 'satisfy' some needs of you and of the world around you.

In summary, we could say that Ikigai must include these 4 main areas:

- What you love to do
- Your skills
- What the world needs
- What you get paid for, or you could be

The Ikigai is like a 'compass' which, once discovered, shows you the direction. It has nothing to do with what you 'should' or have been told to do. It's something totally personal and it's only about what you really care about.

Some examples of Ikigai can be:

- Discover a new drug to treat a chronic disease
- Play the piano in front of a huge audience
- Travel to space and pass on your knowledge to the rest of the world

But these are also Ikigai:

- Eat well
- Play sports
- Family and friends

Ikigai, therefore, is not something that only some people with particular gifts or talents possess.

Before starting the exercises, create the right atmosphere. You have to be focused but relaxed at the same time and carry out the activities with the necessary lightness. The discovery of Ikigai is a pleasant journey, do not live it as an obligation to be released as soon as possible. You can take the time you want to do these exercises. You can also decide to leave some time, even days, between one and the other. Ask yourself what is the 'right time' for you. Get ready to find out what gets you out of bed every morning.

What do you like?

The first exercise will help you better understand your tastes, what you really like.

Focus and answer these questions:

What are my favorite books? Why do I like them?

What are my favorite movies? Why?

What are my favorite events / exhibitions or conferences? Why?

For each question write at least 3 examples with the related reasons.

(Maybe you chose them because they are romantic or they contain real 'pearls of wisdom' or because they concern nature).

Now create a 'Register of recurring themes'

Review your answers and write down the topics, words or phrases with similar content that appear multiple times. Write them in the form of key words. They will give you clear clues as to what you really like.

Be grateful

Several studies show that the people who feel the most gratitude in their life, even for simple everyday experiences, are also the happiest ones. Again, what makes us happier and 'grateful' differs from person to person.

Now try to answer this question:

What good experiences have you experienced today that you feel grateful for? Write down 3.

Now focus on this other question:

How did it happen? What does it mean for you? How can you make them reoccur in the future?

These answers will also help you move towards greater awareness and happiness.

Find yourself

Answer the following questions indicating at least 3 examples and the reasons.

What did you like to do as a child? Why did you like it?

What did you like to do at 13? Why?

What did you like to do at 20? Why?

What do you like to do now? Why?

Take your time to review your answers and find the words, themes and ideas that appear most frequently.

Make notes in the Register of recurring issues.

You might find that you have consistently delighted in being outside and lean toward gutsy exercises or that you have consistently adored aiding those in trouble or those more youthful than you or that you have consistently cherished learning new things and understanding books.

What is your dream?

This is the time to figure out what your current dream is. To find out, there are some questions and 'tricks' that can help you.

Imagine that you are a character you admire, famous or not. The important thing is that he is a person you like very much and who, in your eyes, has exceptional gifts.

What would you do if you had all his skills and means, financial or otherwise?

Compare this answer with those of the previous exercises. You may notice that some dreams, projects, or things that you enjoyed doing in the past no longer have the same meaning for you today. If you still have doubts, try to reread the lists you created and 'feel', with your heart, which ones still have real meaning for you today. Erase the others without fear. It could be goals that you have already accomplished or that are no longer as important to you.

Now ask yourself:

If you were sure you could succeed, what project (s) would you undertake?

If you have made it this far, the answers to these questions will already constitute in themselves a very important key to finding your

Ikigai.

Fill in the graph of your Ikigai

Thanks to the previous exercises and the register of recurring topics, you should be able to fill in the 4 areas described at the beginning. Some of the items you will insert within the diagram may contain elements from 2 different areas. In this case, insert them in the place closest to the 2 areas. As you can see from the diagram, 'intersections' will be created which represent your 'passion', 'mission', 'profession' and 'vocation'. The 'boundaries' of this pattern are fluid and can evolve over time. In fact, your mission could (if not already) become a profession. And so on.

The central intersection, of course, is the most important. It's what makes you get out of bed every morning. Yes, you got it right, it is the Ikigai.

What if Ikigai is still not so clear within your pattern and in your mind? Remember one thing: even research can be so beautiful and so important in your life that it represents your Ikigai itself.

It is an interesting discovery path that leads to an ever greater awareness of ourselves and of our life.

DISCOVERING IKIGAI IS A PATH

In search of your Ikigai, or meaning of life

'Gently surrender to the attraction of the things you love. They will never lead you astray.' Rumi

CHAPTER 4
WHY CAN'T WE FIND OUR IKIGAI?

Each individual is unique and unrepeatable, as is his Ikigai. So why can't everyone find it?

We often get stuck, we limit ourselves, as we fear the judgment of others.

We can be our own most severe judges, mentally repeating to ourselves that "we are ridiculous to hope or dream this or that".

There are a lot of limiting beliefs related to our culture, to the environment, to the fact that we can hurt or disappoint the people we love, that, every day, prevent us from fulfilling ourselves.

We tend to take a successful model and try to emulate it, defining a successful idea that is good for that person, but may not be for us.

By doing this you move away from your true self, from your core values and you begin to generate anxiety, stress, guilt, and feed different fears until you recognize symptoms in your body, such as insomnia.

Welcome the "discomfort" into your life, this will be what will allow you to make bold decisions and embrace change in your life!

That's right, because finding and pursuing your Ikigai doesn't mean "just" feeling fulfilled and happy.

There is so much more.

Because when you are in a state of mind of realization, you are happy and you feel fulfilled, allowing enthusiasm to guide your life, and you are also able to enjoy more good health.

In fact, Japan is one of the longest-lived populations in the world.

It is important to have a healthy diet, keep fit with regular exercise and look for your Ikigai to improve your quality of life.

After all, if your life is happy and meaningful, you already have an intrinsic motivation to do your best to take care of yourself!

Drawing on ancient Japanese wisdom, we can convince ourselves that there is a deeper reason that transcends our everyday life, where every life has its own meaning and its own mission.

In short, everything that happens to us has its own reason, pushing us and orienting us to find our Sense of Life.

When we lose contact with our true selves, we begin to feel a deep sense of incompleteness, of inner emptiness, feeling frustrated and often leading to developing real pathologies such as depression.

Whenever we repress our nature, our character, our creativity, especially if in order to adapt to the expectations of others, we are in fact distancing ourselves from ourselves.

Happiness requires the courage to devote oneself to one's own profound meaning, beyond the opinion and judgments of others.

And to do that, we need to rediscover the courage to be imperfect and vulnerable and to rediscover our true worth, increasing and strengthening our self-esteem.

It is mistakenly thought that living a happy and fulfilling life is equivalent to saying that you have to live a life without problems, without difficulties, where you always have everything you want.

It seems absurd, but it is often the case. If you ask someone what they would like to do in their life, you will probably hear them say that their highest aspiration is to do nothing from morning to night.

Here, these people even with all the money in the world will always be unhappy.

The true joy of living comes from within us, from our creative abilities, from the challenges we set ourselves, from the progress and goals we achieve.

There will be highs, however there will likewise be loads of lows and that is fine. They are both fundamental, but happiness doesn't have to depend on what's outside of us.

You can be happy despite everything.

Because this is a choice, and each of us has the power to choose in which mental and emotional state he wishes to spend every moment of his life.

If on the one hand we have seen how finding our Ikigai allows us to find a higher sense of fulfillment, on the other hand those who live their life with extreme passion risk being consumed by it.

As always, wisdom resides in the middle, in balance, finding the right compromises.

1. Start small

We need to learn to define what the goal is, for example: climbing a mountain.

And then proceed gradually, by breaking down the objectives more and more, until they are transformed into small daily actions that together will lead you, one step after another, to the destination you want.

Remember: it is always better to start small than to face titanic challenges and get discouraged.

2. Forget about yourself

Once you have defined your destination, try to forget about the results you want to achieve and enjoy the journey.

Experience first-hand what it means to be carried away and let things happen around you, as you continue to move forward.

3. Harmony and sustainability

In your path you will always have to remember that your every decision and every action will always have consequences.

Not only for you, but also for the people who are close to you.

Therefore, take into account our personal responsibility not only that we have over our life, but also how we influence what surrounds us.

Adopt a positive attitude to life and seek your harmony and sustainability in doing what you love in a positive way where everyone can benefit.

4. Have joy in the little things

Many times I have tried to emphasize the healing and regenerating power of gratitude.

It really is a great exercise because it allows you to expand your awareness of yourself and your surroundings and how it affects you.

How many times do you really say 'thank you' for that cup of coffee, or the breakfast you make? If it's a beautiful day, can you notice it and express gratitude?

Become a researcher of reasons to be grateful. Life will reward you by giving you more and more!

5. Being in the here and now

By exercising the power of gratitude every day, you will be training yourself to be more aware and mentally present in the here and now.

It is in the present that you are living, every moment of your life is unique, it is up to you to choose how to take advantage of this time. Einstein said that spending 1 minute being angry was equivalent to losing 60 seconds of happiness.

As sad as it may seem, remember that our life always has a

deadline and every moment brings us closer to it.

30 years equals 438,000 hours, which means we have 8,760 hours every year.

How are you investing them?

The Ikigai will reveal itself to you as the perfect intersection of 4 simple elements:

- What you love to do
- What you are good at
- That thing that could bring about positive change in the world
- What you can make a living with

These will be your cardinal points, the parameters that will allow you to guide you in the search for your life purpose.

How to find your Ikigai: 4 questions

To find the 4 fundamental elements that will determine your Ikigai, try to answer these questions:

- What is it that you love more than anything else?
- What are you good at and can you easily improve?
- Which of these things are you good enough to get paid for, no matter what others might think?
- How can you help others, what need could you satisfy, thus making your own contribution to making this beautiful world

better?

If you answered the questions with an open heart, free from your own prejudices and limiting beliefs, then you may already have found the answer and therefore, your Ikigai.

Or maybe, you have an idea, you know which direction to follow, but you still have to define precisely which is your Ikigai.

If you haven't understood it yet, don't worry.

Allow life to take its course and events to happen.

That time has probably not yet come.

What is certain is that by asking yourself these questions, you have set your brain in motion and in particular, your subconscious mind, which will continue to act and seek the best answer for you.

In this way, one beautiful morning while you are taking a shower, or while you are having breakfast, or in general when you feel relaxed, you could see a sudden light and have a clear idea of what your Ikigai is.

In any case, I would like to give you one last practical tip that could help you.

To find the answer to what we are looking for, it can often be useful to go back in time to when we were children.

See what your favorite games were, what you loved doing, what you found easy to do and what you did well.

Find out what your innate abilities are when you were a

completely spontaneous and natural creature, without therefore absorbing all the beliefs and mental constructs of adults.

What did you overlook among your passions and interests when you were a child?

Train your creativity: try to give yourself to drawing, writing, modeling clay, inventing new recipes, building something with Lego, dancing or singing. In short, express yourself in all your forms, only in this way will you be able to really understand what you like and what you don't like to do!

Even if we have some indications, in the end, we proceed by trial and error, making mistakes and always learning something new and more useful to correct the course!

So, never give up and find your Ikigai!

CHAPTER 5
IKIGAI AND FLOW

What do we seek? What do we really want? What makes us happy and grateful to be in the world?

Exploring the fascinating Japanese concept of Ikigai, I came across Kamiya Mieko the psychiatrist who in 1966 wrote and divulged Ikigai in a text which kicked off the spread of the term and the reflection that followed in Japan and which continues to this day.

It took him 7 years to write this book because it contains all his long experience of supporting people with Hansen's disease that made people feel aimless, insignificant, like nothing.

Hence his broad reflection on the theme that indicates quality and not quantity, as the main parameter to generate the sense of one's reason for living: to evaluate and deepen even the shortest portion of life that one has available, passing from the struggle to do not succumb to "that something that makes you think it was worth living".

Ikigai is in fact the Japanese term to indicate the raison d'etre of human existence, investigated by many philosophers and thinkers, which here takes on characteristics very close to savoring life as a child who is happy without knowing why, without setting goals, happy in what he is trying his hand at, in the flow of his playing and living.

Basically the Ikigai (the raison d'etre and the vital drive) is realized when what you want coincides with what is right, is good, must be done.

It is something that in fact includes others, which increases and strengthens precisely when one shares, gives oneself, amplifying the value of the impact.

Ikigai has a lot to do with the person, with his essence, and does not depend on the things you do or the situation in which you live, but manifests itself in the connection between the inside of the person and the outside that intercepts it and with which it merges: it belongs to each of us, and always remains with us, if we are able to continue to see it.

To see it you need to distance yourself from the ego, from the vision that contains only the self in order to broaden your point of view and observe carefully and patiently: like when you lose something in the water and the more you move it, the more difficult it is to see clearly, while as soon as you stop and the water calms down, everything is seen more clearly and you find what you had lost sight of.

Contact with nature, constant commitment, taking care of people, things and the environment, the joy of meeting and sharing with others are the elements that Kamiya Mieko pointed to get closer to finding her own Ikigai. This is why the utilitarian version with which the Ikigai then spread throughout the world has partly betrayed the original meaning.

For us Westerners it can be useful to stop and ask ourselves in any case the typical questions proposed by the Ikigai icon whose intertwining can help us connect with ourselves and our reason for being and living, to venture into an exploration that brings up so much of what is already in us, so that it can be available to all:

- What do I love? (my passion)
- What does the world need? (my mission)
- What am I good at? (my calling)
- What can I be paid for? (my sustainability)

The common graphic representation of the Ikigai as we know it, shows at the center of these responses a space of equilibrium which corresponds to the vital drive, the raison d'etre of each one, the personal purpose that characterizes us.

This is why it becomes so important to know that Ikigai is already part of us, each one has this point of balance between what he loves, what he knows how to do well, what the world needs, what makes this gift sustainable.

The translation of this concept in a Western key is precisely that of discovering one's talents, developing them, offering them to the world and being happy to cultivate them for the common good.

When this balance is in action, we realize it because we experience activities in which we lose track of time, in which we are immersed in a state of deep concentration, presence, calm and pleasure that is called flow.

Basically, flow is the way we put our Ikigai into action and we have all experienced it in life.

It is therefore important to spend time with discipline to practice connecting with your Ikigai and bring it into our daily life by experiencing the flow, that state of grace when we are fully present in the moment and activity we are experiencing.

In the same way, experiencing the flow can offer us indications to give answers to the questions that guide us to discover our Ikigai.

So when we do the work we love, we are aware of the fact that we are carrying out a task that is important and demanding for us, so much so that it requires our attention in tranquility and with the full energy available, we eliminate all distractions and have fun in the discipline of what we do, we are making sure that we will eventually reap rewards for ourselves and for others.

Isn't this the fantastic experience of the game that we have all experienced: serious, committed, fun, focused, which involved us in the relationship with others until the end of everyone's pleasure and satisfaction, and then resumed with renewed energy?

Who among us has never experienced the feeling of being completely absorbed in an activity to the point of forgetting everything around him, without even noticing the passage of time? This state of absolute concentration is called flow and is the key to achieving maximum productivity.

WHAT IS THE STATE OF FLOW?

The concept of flow, or state of flow, also known as competitive trance in sports, was first described in 1975 by the psychologist Mihaly Csikszentmihalyi and further analyzed in his book Flow: The Psychology of Optimal Experience. In the years following the publication of Csikszentmihalyi 's text, the concept of flow has spread to areas such as sport, music, education and has even found application in the field of religion and spirituality, given its proximity to the concept of mindfulness, central to the Buddhist religion, Zen philosophy and yoga meditation practices.

According to Csikszentmihalyi 's description, the state of flow is characterized by an intense concentration focused on the present moment, a total harmony between thought and action, a feeling of competence and absolute control over the experience, accompanied by a distortion of the perception of time and gives a deep sense of gratification and well-being. And it is precisely this sensation of intense well-being that makes it possible to reach the maximum peak in terms of performance, creativity and productivity, without effort and almost without feeling fatigue.

REACHING THE STATE OF FLOW

Most of us are able to reach the state of flow quite spontaneously, especially when we are engaged in activities that we consider enjoyable and stimulating. However, given the enormous benefits of doing any activity while in this state of grace, it is not surprising that many wish to reach this state of mind voluntarily, in order to be able to give the best of themselves in work, but also in sport or in private life.

But is it possible to enter the flow state 'on command'? According to Leo Babauta, author of a popular blog called Zenhabits that deals with productivity and time management, getting into flow takes just a little practice. Here's where to start:

Choose a stimulating activity. If we have to dedicate ourselves to a job we hate to do, it will be much more difficult, if not impossible, to reach the state of flow, but this does not mean that the flow is only possible during activities we love: often a change of perspective is enough to make it interesting, or at least stimulating, an activity that so far we have considered unpleasant.

Dedicate yourself to something important. To practice reaching the state of flow, we choose a project that stimulates our curiosity and our interest, but which is at the same time relevant to our career or professional growth: boredom is the worst enemy of flow.

Choose the right level of difficulty. As difficult as it may be to balance, in order to reach the state of flow it is essential that the activity we choose is neither too easy nor too difficult. If it is too simple a task, it will not be necessary to maintain concentration to complete it, while if it is too complex we would end up using a large part of our energies and our concentration just to understand how to approach the task.

Banish interruptions and distractions. On this blog we have talked several times about the cost of interruptions in terms of productivity and the negative effect of distractions on our concentration, so it is essential to be able to remove any source of distraction, if our goal is to learn to voluntarily enter a state of flow.

Practice and be patient. Especially for those who are used to working constantly switching from one job to another, it may be very difficult at first to focus on a single activity, but abandoning the multitasking mentality is essential to be able to reach the state of flow. Luckily, learning to focus is primarily a matter of patience - progressive training can produce amazing results in no time.

The flow state is one of the keys to happiness in both work and private life, and a side benefit of it is that it not only reduces stress, but increases productivity dramatically. Flow is in fact a state of mind that roots us entirely in the present and helps us to be more creative, productive and happy. Not bad huh?

This state of awareness tends to manifest itself when a person pays full attention to a task that he performs for intrinsic reasons, i.e. the person carries out the activity for himself, rather than as a means to an end. This activity completely attracts the person's attention, so that the mind is totally absorbed in what it is doing.

When you are in the state of flow, your entire being is immersed in activity and everything seems to be working together in complete harmony. Your performance level is often at its peak, reaching the optimum level of creativity, clarity and concentration without any effort. You are not evaluating every move, nor are you planning your next move. In the flow, your ego withdraws, leaving room for the process, unimpeded: you are not aware of inhibitions, hunger, thirst, fatigue, aches or anything outside of activity. All worries, thoughts and memories seem to dissolve. Time flies, but you will be completely unaware of it, as if you were out of it for the moment. In the flow you become one with what you are doing.

In summary, when we enter the flow state:

- We are completely immersed in what we are doing
- We forget about ourselves, others and the outside world
- We lose track of time
- We feel happy and in control
- We become creative and productive
- We enjoy doing what we are doing
- Our performance is at the highest level

Mihaly Csikszentmihalyi, the first who described this concept in his book, "Flow: the psychology of optimal experience", often describes flow as an autotelic experience. An autotelic experience simply describes an activity that is enjoyable in itself, fun, and inherently motivating. It also suggests that we can apply flow status to nearly all of our business fields. In his words, we could say that "in the state of flow the ego is annulled, there is no separation between the performer and the activity itself, and time literally flies. You feel part of something bigger, every action or thought inevitably follows from the previous one, you act and think to the best of your ability, without external interference and without particular efforts."

What can be deduced from these words is that the state of flow applies the Zen concept of living completely in the present moment to the productive environment: in fact, we speak of being totally present to oneself, being completely concentrated on a single activity and finding a sense of calm, happiness and fulfillment in the act of getting the job done. The flow state is exactly that.

The ability to focus on a single task (as opposed to multiple tasks) is one of the keys to true productivity - that kind of productivity where you actually accomplish your goals. The flow state has nothing to do with the artificial concept of productivity in which 10 tasks are eliminated from the to-do-list at a time.

If you spend your days jumping from one activity to another, trying to carry out your work through multitasking, you will hardly be able to focus on what really matters.

True productivity leads us to accomplish important and lasting things. It means completing key projects rather than answering dozens of emails, making a lot of conference calls and attending a lot of meetings. It means completing key activities. It means quality rather than quantity. And once you have learned to focus on these kinds of important projects and activities, the flow state is how you do them: it allows you to fully immerse yourself in these kinds of activities and ignore the rest, so that you stay focused on these tasks long enough to actually complete them.

How to enter the flow state

Given these assumptions, it would seem interesting to understand how to reach the state of flow in one's daily life. So let's get into it more: how can we get this mystical state that makes us more productive and happier? Should we meditate or study Zen philosophy? As much as meditation can help, it is not absolutely necessary. And the state of flow is anything but mystical - it's very practical and achieving it is no secret to a select few. It may take practice, sure, but over time it will get easier and easier. We will now see what are the main triggers that trigger the flow state, and then a series of key steps to achieve flow in our daily life.

The flow state triggers

Psychological triggers

Intense concentration - concentration is really intense when we focus with undivided attention on a single task.

Clarity of objectives - the objective we are working towards must be clear and unambiguous, that is, it must be a SMART objective. In this way our mind can fully dedicate itself to the activity we are doing without wondering what the next step could be.

Immediate Feedback - immediate feedback means aligning our awareness and attention, so we can precisely evaluate what we're doing.

Challenge-to-skill ratio - too demanding tasks can make us feel overwhelmed, unequipped and anxious. A too simple task, on the other hand, can lead us to an attitude of sufficiency. To trigger the flow, a target should be somewhere between these two extremes.

Environmental triggers

Sense of Danger - our focus is instinctively increased when we detect a sense of danger in our environment. This sense of danger refers to the subjective perception of each one: for some it might be speaking publicly, for others, to approach another person.

New and complex environments - when we find ourselves in new, complex, dynamic or unpredictable environments, our attention is enhanced. On the other hand, in environments of this type we are more likely to be distracted because of new and interesting stimuli.

Creative triggers

Creativity - flow triggers creativity, that triggers the flow, that empowers creativity, that empowers the flow ... and so on in a domino effect.

Key steps to achieve flow state

We just saw what the main triggers are for triggering the flow state. Now the question is: what can I do, operationally speaking, to enter the flow state? As you may have already guessed, there is no single answer that works for everyone: different people react differently to different stimuli. What we can do, however, is to list a series of essential key steps, to be adjusted according to your habits or inclinations.

Choose a job you love

If you don't like your current job, you will have great difficulty in reaching the state of flow. This is a sad truth. If you fear an activity, or if you are annoyed while completing it, getting lost in it will be practically impossible. If your work is only made up of things you hate, the real question isn't 'how to get to the state of flow?' but 'why haven't you changed it yet?' But it is more likely that there are things in your work that you love to do: so if you want to reach the state of flow, the first step is to dedicate yourself to projects that you are passionate about.

Choose an important task

Make sure it's challenging, but not too difficult

Find your moment

Find a quiet time in your day when you have a lot of energy and can focus. It could be early in the morning, as soon as you wake up, or you could try the lunch break, or even the evening hours, it depends a lot on the type of person you are. In any case, whatever time you choose, it should also be a time of peak energy - times when you feel tired are never good for reaching the state of flow.

Eliminate distractions

Once you've found your moment, you'll need to find your place.

To get into the flow you need to work in a quiet place away from interruptions and distractions. That means turning off your phone, email notifications, turning off sites like Facebook or Twitter, and anything else that might interrupt your thoughts. Furthermore, as we explained in the article on how to organize your work, it is very useful to clean your desk of objects that you do not need: a clean and minimal work environment helps immensely.

Think positive and manage your stress

It is very difficult to concentrate if you have negative thoughts in your mind. Also, negativity often undermines the way we approach work, people and problems, making everything more difficult. Therefore, if you want to improve your ability to concentrate it is necessary to clear your mind from worries, anxieties, negative thinking and, in general, from stress. Identify your main sources of stress by keeping a daily "stress diary" and then work on eliminating the biggest ones. Meditation is a prodigious tool for managing these things: if you want to learn more, read our article on meditation as a productivity tool.

Learn to focus on one activity for as long as possible

No more multitasking! You need to start the business of your choice and focus on it for as long as possible. This takes practice. After some practice, you will definitely be better off. If you can focus on this task long enough without distraction, and if this task has been chosen well (something you love, something important, and something challenging but not too difficult), you should quickly reach the state of flow.

Have a good time

Experiencing flow is a great thing. It's really nice to be able to pour all of yourself into something interesting and useful, make great progress on an important project, do something you are passionate about: at the end of the day, take the time to appreciate this feeling.

Keep practicing

Each step will require some practice to be 100% effective: finding your moment, eliminating distractions, choosing the right task. And above all, the fact that you focus on one activity for a long time. You will fail often, but it doesn't matter: every time you fail, try to understand where you can improve and every time you succeed, try to understand what you have done better than at other times. And the more you train, the more you will improve.

Reap the rewards

Getting into the flow state is pleasant in itself, but it has a truly amazing side effect: you'll be happier with your work in general as well. This is because the flow state allows you to complete more things and more often, get better and better results, and get better and better at what you do. Take the time to appreciate it and to continue practicing it every day.

CHAPTER 6
THE MANDALA

The term "mandala" comes from Sanskrit and literally means "disk" or in any case it refers to a shape with a center from which shapes radiate. The mandala exists both in square and circular form and the designs inside it can be simple or very complex; these are shapes that are often repeated with harmony and expand from the center towards the outside.

The circular shape refers to the circle of life and represents the force of existence understood as a radiating source of creation. The geometric design in the East supports both meditation and prayers and strengthens the intention. In the sacred Buddhist tradition, monks make mandalas as sand constructions. Finely embroidered or painted or drawn mandalas serve the practitioner as a guide to go to the center of oneself but also to connect to the universe and its harmonically perfect laws. To make the mandala in an artisanal way, even random round shapes are enough, such as the lid of a jar or other round shapes to which the tip of a pencil is placed; It is also advisable to find them of different sizes in order to make small and large concentric circles well. In other cases, a compass also works very well. We also recommend trying to trace freehand, the feeling pays off a lot even if the circles may be slightly imperfect.

The power that increases by continuing to repeat the geometric shapes corresponds to a power of the person on the spiritual, emotional, practical, rational level. It is a kind of reset that also releases stress in an active and fruitful way, helping to return to the full power of one's positive feelings. By making a mandala we return to reflect on our place in the world and on how we feel we inhabit our body and our creative spirit. There are immediate results and it is a real small ceremony.

The value of this gesture has a strongly purifying character and brings us back to the fact that from the center of our being we project who we are and that for this reason it is convenient to constantly take care of our emotions. The mandala corresponds in all respects to a real journey within ourselves.

Even the choice of colors, shapes (drop, arch, etc) are real ways to get in touch with your soul, especially when the mental aspect is silenced a little. In the classical meaning of the mandala also the colors have a meaning (yellow the awareness, the blue the maternal sense, the red the vital impulse etc) as well as the shapes (square rational aspect, triangle direction, point or circle the center and the expansion). Very often numbers with precise symbols were also represented in the mandalas. There are specific forms of mandalas that can also be found online with an explanation of their effect on the soul and on those who trace them; even trying to draw one of these models has its effect, although moving without a trace or pattern leaves many unpredictable paths open to one's inner world.

The benefits

Whatever state of emotion runs through us, making a mandala helps to refocus and go through that given emotional wave. When you are experiencing a moment of sadness or great transformation, making a mandala helps to gather energy and deeply see the mood that inhabits it. Emotions are freed and expressed in making the mandala. Carl Jung was responsible for introducing the mandala in the psychological field; the scholar, after having deepened its meaning, defined the mandala as the symbolic representation of emotions.

Finally, there are many books with forms that refer to the mandala that can be colored in moments of general relaxation and idleness: doing so helps to release tensions and remain in connection with one's center, it serves to detach the mind and also activate the inner child. While doing the mandala, our whole being is concentrated in the full power of its resources. There is a great release of tension and negative thoughts accumulated about others or about ourselves. In doing so we can also look clearly at our inner world of that given moment, our patterns, our fears. In many traditions, making the mandala serves precisely to break many fears and to remove obstacles that slow us down or prevent our own realization.

Very often the mandala hangs for a given time (1 day or 2 or even a week, depending on the goal) in a quiet place, not where you sleep, and it burns at the right time and perhaps with the appropriate moon. Burning means removing, making sacred everything that helps us to grow and evolve. Once done, the mandala in other cases is not burned, but kept in a safe place so that it continues to produce its effects and reminds us of an important part of the our path. The mandala puts us in strong contact with our soul and the only gesture of tracing shapes, and especially a central circle, helps us to project ourselves / and into a sacred boundary, remembering our nature, itself sacred.

CHAPTER 7
WABI SABI

Each culture has its own philosophy of life. If the Swedish Lagom pushes to accept compromise, the middle ways, moderation as a way for an inner balance, in Scotland the Coorie instead presupposes that one finds happiness in one's daily life, made up of peaceful walks among cliffs and woods, evenings at the pubs and fireplaces as the storm rages outside. The Japanese Wabi Sabi, on the other hand, applies the Zen approach of the Japanese to life.

Wabi Sabi is nothing more than a vision founded on the acceptance of the transience and imperfection of life.

Know your limits and accept them

Within this philosophy, many concepts from esoteric Tantric Buddhism, Zen philosophy and Taoism. A combination that leads to accepting one's own weaknesses, anxieties and fears. To learn more, there are many books, including that of Selene Calloni Williams: Wabi Sabi. The beauty of imperfect life. The Japanese way to be happy that starts from a fundamental concept for this philosophy: the knowledge of not knowing.

In a world, ours, where it seems to us that we must always have everything under control and we find it difficult to let go, Wabi Sabi can be liberating.

Among the essential principles of this philosophy of life is to be aware that we cannot control everything, that we cannot know everything, that it will be inevitable to make mistakes sooner or later. But that all this must not be a limit not to do, on the contrary, one must always move and get involved, however aware of one's own limits. Having reached this awareness gives a person great strength because it frees him from fears and above all from the anxieties of failing. A concept extremely far from the Western one, which has always based its culture since the past centuries on the search for success and on the idea that everything is eternal.

How to apply it in daily life

How to put Wabi Sabi into practice then? Starting to work on this concept: living aware of personal limitations, slowing down to enjoy even the little things, appreciate the present better and not think too much about the future which, according to Japanese philosophy, generates too many anxieties. In other words, also learn to let go.

Why believe in Wabi Sabi, the Japanese principle according to which beauty lies in imperfection

An ancient word with a spiritual meaning. Wabi -Sabi is a sincere way of seeing the world and living life as it is, and we should all experience it

Buddhist philosophy has now become a part of our Western culture for several years. Thanks to disciplines such as yoga and meditation, or Tibetan art, we Europeans too are no longer strangers to the introspective thought typical of Buddhism.

Let's start from the etymology of the Japanese word, composed of wabi , which means poverty, simplicity. And sabi, which indicates the beauty born of the passage of time. Wabi sabi is a Japanese aesthetic conception founded on the acceptance of the imperfection and impermanence of things. It is often associated with antiques: antique objects and tools of great value, often worn, broken in some places, yet for this very reason wonderful.

Taken from Buddhist teachings, this principle is therefore based on the search for beauty in imperfections and incompleteness. In other words, it means accepting the transience and asymmetry in our lives. According to the Buddhist current of thought, this way of life can guide us towards a simpler and more fulfilling existence. The Japanese writer Okakura Tenshin , known as Okakura Kakuzo , in his book The Book of Tea, first published in 1902, wrote that the word wabi translates the meaning of imperfect very well. While sabi represents the deteriorated state of the objects. Physicist and author Terada Torajiko , on the other hand, described this word as “the beauty that transpires from the inside of an ancient thing, but which has nothing to do with appearance. For example, a rock covered with moss has this beauty ”.

When and how to use the word " wabi sabi"

Accepting who we are and grasping the taste of small daily details is not easy. But living according to the wabi -sabi culture really means adopting existential strategies that promote the nature of being and of the natural becoming of things. Repairing objects, rather than throwing them out and buying new ones, for example, is an action imbued with wabi sabi. That ancient chipped vase of the great-grandmother, perhaps, has a very long story that is worth telling.

Where is a lot of beauty even in a flower when it is wilted, not just when it is fresh and lush

There is a lot of beauty even in a flower when it is wilted, not just when it is fresh and lush. The expression wabi sabi is a way of living life and looking at reality that gives value to what would otherwise be considered lost, wrong, without power. The charm of the antique, the rustic and the rough, an elegance that shows itself without being intrusive, a concept of beauty aware of the natural change of events and people, who age without generating melancholy.

A journey can learn about wabi sabi. When we leave to (re) find ourselves, when on the way we accept to lose ourselves, to experience solitude and silence, and thus we are able to grasp all its value. A wabi -sabi activity is a meditation, a physical and mental practice to regain the balance of the breath.

Wabi sabi is the little things, it is the acceptance of time that passes inexorably and cannot be stopped. It is a wrinkle under the eyes, a scar that makes us unique, a shy and reserved way of communicating that hides depth and goodness of soul.

wabi sabi philosophy every day with ourselves, with others, with the situations we live in, with the objects we surround ourselves with.

Why do we need it

If we think of the evolution of the history of art over the centuries, it is not difficult to notice that the periods of research of classical beauty, imperturbable, perfect and eternal, are always followed by contrasting artistic currents. Let's think of the 19th century European aesthetic trend that goes beyond with the arrival of Romanticism: melancholy, nostalgia, abandonment, poignant and imperfect beauty, popular themes become the favorite subjects of the artists of the time. The previous Greek sculptures, balance and symmetry give way to a much truer and more sincere reality.

Romanticism is perhaps the most concrete meeting point between Europe and Japan. In the Rising Sun, the harmony of things comes precisely from a simplicity in the forms and representations that leave room for melancholy, nostalgia, the most delicate sadness .

It is not trivial to stop and appreciate the real and tangible imperfection that not only characterizes things, but also - and above all - human beings. If we left more room for this, we would find that perfectionism is a disease that brings only distress and despair. If we allowed our eyes and our hearts to see and hear wabi -sabi, perhaps, we would see the beauty that was previously invisible and intangible to us.If you asked a Japanese to define the term " wabi -sabi" (侘寂), he would probably just shake his head hesitantly, unable to put into words the wabi -sabi sensation.

But what, then, does wabi -sabi mean?

For many Japanese critics, wabi -sabi is something that can never really be understood, and that should keep this aura of mystery and elusiveness, as its ineffability is just what makes it special.

Trying to define wabi -sabi without altering or diminishing its nature is practically impossible. Leonard Koren , artist, writer and expert in Japanese aesthetics, tried it, as well as one of the first to have introduced the concept of wabi -sabi in Western aesthetics, after having discovered and learned it during a personal "spiritual search".

Wanting to give it a broad definition, we could say that wabi -sabi is a lifestyle, a particular type of aesthetic conception, of beauty.

" Rustic", "rough", are the words that are usually used to describe the first impression after seeing an expression of wabi -sabi, although they represent only a limited dimension of the word.

The metaphysical, spiritual and moral principles behind the wabi -sabi concept derive from ideas of simplicity, naturalness and acceptance of reality, ideas found in Chinese Zen Buddhism and Taoism. The term derives from that atmosphere of desolation and melancholy, from the minimalism found in Chinese poetry and monochromatic paintings of the ninth and tenth centuries.

Throughout history, although the wabi -sabi concept permeated almost every aspect of sophisticated Japanese culture, it has found its highest expression in the tea ceremony. The latter goes beyond the simple preparation of a drink, but it is a ceremony that combines various skills and areas: architecture, interior and garden design, floral creations, painting, preparation of dishes and much more.

The truth comes from observing nature

Nature is unpredictable, especially the one that often violently overwhelms the Land of the Rising Sun: earthquakes, eruptions, typhoons, floods. The Japanese have tried to control it as far as possible, and have learned from it.

The "Greatness" is found in the imperceptible and neglected details

Wabi -sabi does not find himself in lush and blooming nature, but in what has just been created, or in what is about to disappear. It is found in the details, in the ephemeral, in what is invisible to ordinary eyes. To experience the wabi -sabi, you have to slow down, be patient, look closely.

Focus on the intrinsic and ignore the material hierarchy

wabi -sabi tea room are a clear expression of the wabi -sabi values. As a symbolic act of humility, all who enter the hall must crouch or crawl, passing through a specially created small and low door. Once inside the tea room, all the participants are the same, no hierarchical system is acceptable inside, not even referring to the material value of things. In wabi -sabi there is no such thing as "precious", as this would imply the existence of something "not precious". An object assumes the wabi -sabi state only when it is appreciated as such.

Wabi - sabi things bear the marks of time, climate and humane treatment. They show their vulnerability to the action of the sun, wind, rain, cold, visible signs in their spots, cracks, discolorations, deformations. Although these things are very fragile, on the verge of dematerializing (or materializing), they still possess a certain resolve and a strong presence.

Wabi - sabi things differ from conventional tastes: they appear strange, misshapen, curious or, for many people, just plain ugly. A broken bowl whose pieces have been glued together is a good example.

Wabi - sabi things are usually small and compact, they project us inward. The wabi -sabi spaces are secluded, private, intimate. They are peaceful and soothing, like a welcoming and enveloping mother's womb.

Wabi - sabi things don't ask to be the center of attention, they are humble and modest, but not without presence or silent authority. They are only appreciated through direct contact and use. They do not need to establish themselves in the market culture, nor to have confirmation of their status or that of their creator. In fact, their creator is best not distinguishable, invisible or anonymous.

Wabi - sabi things usually come from earth materials, used in their original state. They are characterized by rough textures, rough to the touch. They have "muted" qualities, such as bright colors that fade into earth tones, sunrise and sunset, or vary across a broad scale of grays and browns. Sometimes, wabi -sabi things have pastel colors associated with something that has just emerged from nowhere, just blossomed.

Simplicity is the essence of wabi -sabi.

Nothingness represents extreme, ultimate simplicity. But finding it before or after nowhere is not easy.

How to achieve simplicity without leading to ostentatious austerity? How to pay attention to details without becoming obsessed with them? How to achieve simplicity while avoiding boredom?

The simplicity of wabi -sabi can be described as a state of grace achieved by a sober, modest, sincere intelligence.

Wabi -sabi is surrounding oneself with modest, but not sterile things (wabi -sabi things give off warmth on an emotional level, not coldness).

Wabi -sabi is to reduce everything to the essence, without removing the poetry.

Enjoy the here and now. Being resilient, accepting that things can change and embracing this change without fighting it. Above all, be aware that not everything is in our hands, that we can lose in life and that situations can get out of hand. All this is Wabi Sabi, the

Japanese philosophy that leads to accepting life for what it is, enjoying every single moment.

Imagine a book with yellowed pages and a slightly wrinkled cover, perhaps with some stains. A classic text passed from hand to hand, from parents to children, which now remains in the home library waiting to be picked up by some new story enthusiast. Those defects due to time and wear make the book a unique piece, able to evoke unforgettable moments and, for this reason, increase its beauty. This, in short, is the Japanese wabi-sabi: the ability to welcome and understand the beauty of imperfection.

Wabi-sabi: two words for one concept

Two distinct terms which, together, explain a precise concept. Wabi indicates discreet beauty, born of natural and never intentional imperfection. A typical example is an object that is the result of craftsmanship: beauty is given precisely by the small defects that indicate manual processing.

Sabi, on the other hand, expresses an idea of beauty linked to the passage of time that is revealed only with wear and tear due to aging. An example? Grandma's silver cutlery, whose stains no longer go away or an antique piece of furniture, with new cracks in the wood.

Wabi-sabi, therefore, goes beyond appearance to focus on the subtlest levels and the less obvious aspects, drawing inspiration from nature for its fundamental rules: nothing is perfect, nothing is complete, nothing is permanent. Not surprisingly, wabi-sabi objects at first sight appear asymmetrical, simple, made with natural materials, with irregular surfaces, of uneven color: it is necessary to have experience and a superior sensitivity to fully appreciate their aesthetic value. The only way to experience wabi-sabi is to turn the attention from the outside to the inside.

The concept of wabi-sabi applies to all areas of existence: from art to photography, from nature to social relations, from furniture to work. You just have to practice.

Beauty and imperfection, words that put together seem to oppose each other so much that they are almost revolutionary today, but which, nevertheless, are increasingly part of everyday life.

Wabi Sabi is a cardinal principle of the Japanese worldview which, as a lifestyle, method of thought, state of consciousness, summarizes in itself most of the secrets of esoteric Tantric Buddhism, Zen and, even before, Taoism. It is a philosophy that is very successful in the West. Not only as a tool for personal growth, but also as a way to pursue a full and happy existence. The etymological origin of the word "wabi" refers to simplicity, it is melancholy and imperfection. While the word "sabi" represents the passage of time, that which vanishes and never comes back, which invites us to focus on the here and now, without worrying about what will be.

Seeking different points of view to read ourselves and the world around us, making the most of the creative power of our mind can offer us the way to face stress, radical changes or to allow us a new, unexpected but more satisfying direction.

We try to slow down our pace, to live without wanting to control everything. Finding a lifestyle that creates harmony around us and that helps us discover beauty in little things, welcome every moment for what it is and give thanks for what it is giving us. By focusing on the present time, we can gain awareness, enjoy that experience and be happy with it.

But how to put all this into practice? I find it very beneficial in mindfulness, a practice that has taught me to welcome every emotion and to let go of what weighs me down, freeing up space for new ideas and new projects, to develop one's creativity without forgetting the nostalgia of the past moments they do. part of our inner growth.

Let's open our mind, fill it with little miracles and accept our imperfectly perfect life.

CHAPTER 8
LEARNING TO LIVE IN THE HERE AND NOW

Learning to live in the here and now means taking your life in hand, letting go, being present, enjoying every moment of life

We are more and more used to building our existence according to objectives and goals to be achieved, it is we who attribute this value to life, especially in the culture of Western society, but all this is far from the pure and simple truth of things.

Our goals help to better channel the energies, allow us to improve our existence and those around us, they can be a valid contribution to go beyond our limits and know that we can do it. However, encountering difficulties does not mean being punished, just as a good result does not mean that you should feel on the right path.

There is no crossroads of destiny, no train to catch on the fly or the perfect opportunity: there are choices that we make moment by moment. Each of us builds our own story moment by moment: now you are here. what happened yesterday is no longer important, you cannot change it. But you are here, full of life. Right now.

Have you ever noticed that today, very often, a disease (or a pandemic) is the only event capable of making us change our lives? We keep putting off what we love with the excuse of time, the rent, the children: know that there will not come a day when suddenly you will have the time, the means, the possibility to do what you want.

Why let a negative event give us the alarm bell to slow down? It is not about leading a different existence, but about transforming the way you approach life.

STOP AND BREATHE

Practice stopping during the day : just a few seconds and at least 3-4 deep breaths. Feel the air entering and filling your lungs, hold it for a moment then exhale.

If you want you can look at a point of the landscape beyond the window, it will have a restful effect. Or close your eyes if you feel the need to isolate yourself for a moment. Don't be afraid of loneliness. You will find a piece of peace in the confusion. Leave a post it note on the fridge or kitchen cabinet to remind yourself: "Breathe!" Over time you will repeat this simple gesture more and more often, until it becomes a habit: a small ritual that is already meditation. Breath is the first breath with which we come into the world and the last with which we return life. Each moment is unique.

Listen to your needs.

Probably you too do a thousand things every day: work, home

and sometimes children make the days a run-up to the next goal. Often we end up running in such a habitual and mechanical way that we lose sight of our original need. What are your deepest needs ? Take 10 minutes and straight away, on a blank sheet of paper, write down what makes you feel good and smile. Do it now: you can add everything you feel, the important thing is not to think too much and follow your instinct.

From deep situations to a simple flowerpot on the windowsill, your list will tell you a lot about what you need to stay healthy. Hang it on the fridge or on your computer and play this game: every week try to create one of these situations. New places to discover (maybe just thirty minutes by train from home), an hour all to yourself to read or lie down on the sofa, a snack with bread and jam as a child, an afternoon with a friend, the new jar of flowers to take care of: how many things make us smile?

TAKE CARE OF YOUR BODY

Those who go running or cycling regularly know the strange intoxication capable of enveloping the entire body when practicing regular physical activity: the resistance to fatigue increases, the skin oxygenates while the cells absorb the beneficial effects of vitamin D through the light. solar, the body perceives a deep lightness and elasticity, the discharge of endorphins makes us stronger and smiling.

Setting yourself a goal in this case can be useful because it helps to push what we believed to be our limits a little further.

Three songs on the radio while you go wild at home, about twenty minutes walking in the nearby park, a bike ride at sunset: take them as a little exercise to do every day. From morning to evening our body follows us faithfully in every action, yet we often end up considering it a burden, a burden or a nuisance: rarely are we willing to nourish it, care for it and love it with the affection it deserves.

The good night ritual, for example, is always a cuddle. Take a dark shower and while you massage your skin with a natural scented oil, learn every area of your body by touch. Do you know that there are areas that you always rub quickly or do not even touch? There is no age in which to learn to feel what we are. Start from your skin, exercise your sense of smell and taste, discover your true beauty: that is the enthusiasm, curiosity and that charge of passion that lights up each of us when we stop thinking or start smiling at each other.

RELEASE THE EMOTIONS OF THE MOMENT YOU ARE LIVING

The custom of five o'clock tea had some important characteristics. For example , sipping a healthy and good drink while sharing your time with friends. Another fundamental point should not be forgotten, namely the opportunity to stop.

Blocking what you are doing for a moment is a small choice that can establish a positive routine. When do you need it for tea? 15 minutes, time to boil the water and let your favorite fragrance rest. Sit down. Feel the heat that goes from the throat to the belly. Breathe, look out the window. You smile. Read a book, let your thoughts run wild, or invite some friends. Just be present: being here and now means not thinking about anything else. While I wash the dishes, I see and think of the dishes, when I sip the tea I practice savoring it and feeling what my body feels: your emotions flow freely, the head stops thoughts, the breath becomes deep. Your heart is beating, right now, every moment.

Well-being is created day after day: it is a matter of choice. Start here, learn to slow down and find that quality of life is possible.

CHAPTER 9
ICHIGO ICHIE

The Japanese articulation Ichigo Ichie It can be deciphered as "once, a gathering" or "at this time, an open door", the meaning of both indicates a sort of carpe diem, to remind us that every single moment is unique and we must take advantage of this.

This philosophy, which could recall the principles of mindfulness, for which every moment spent is infinitely precious and for this reason it deserves to be lived with our full awareness.

The act of Ichigo Ichie will permit you to carry on with a more tranquil existence without stresses over the future or without conveying the balance of the past.

The philosophy of Ichigo Ichie can be summarized in 10 principles: try not to put off exceptional minutes: each second is interesting and on the off chance that you don't embrace it is lost for eternity.

live as though this happens just a single time in your life: particularly experiences with companions and friends and family live as though it happens just a single time.

embrace the here and now: you can't change what has occurred and it is pointless to stress over the future since you are don't know of what will occur, so live at the time since all streets are conceivable.

Do something you've never done before: as Einstein said: “we can't expect things to change, always doing the same things”. This is why you cannot make anything new blossom if you do not allow the new to enter you.

Practice meditation: you will simply have to sit on a chair or cushion, close your eyes and breathe. Calm down for a few minutes and let your anxieties, fears and worries flow in favor of well-being.

Consciously apply the 5 senses: listen, look, smell, listen and taste. In every experience you have, remember to use all 5 of your senses. This will allow you to be more attentive to what is going on around you and increase your level of empathy.

Note the coincidences: chance does not exist and if you are looking for answers you should pay attention to the signals that the universe sends you. Keeping a diary where you write down what happens to you could help you.

Turns every day into a party: you don't have to wait for a birthday, an anniversary or a special event to take the opportunity to celebrate and treat yourself to a special day. Treat yourself to these days when you feel like it and with the right frame of mind the ordinary could become extraordinary.

If you don't like what you do, do something different: always taking up the Einstein maxim used previously, remember that if you change you can't get different results. If you feel unhappy in the situation you are experiencing, start making changes. Apply Ichigo Ichie to create a new reality for yourself.

Become a hunter of special moments: the more you train yourself to consider the moments you live as special, the more special moments you will experience.

CHAPTER 10
THE SECRET OF OKINAWA

In the middle of the Pacific, exactly in the China Sea, between Taiwan and the Japanese archipelago, we find Okinawa, the Japanese prefecture which includes over 150 islands. This place is particularly famous for its tropical climate, wide beaches and coral reefs, but also for sites of historical importance that retain traces of the Second World War.

Okinawa, however, is also famous for another thing: this is where the secret of longevity is hidden. It is no coincidence, in fact, that it is precisely the inhabitants of the islands of the archipelago who hold the longevity record compared to the other inhabitants of Japan and the world.

Life expectancy is the highest in the world and there are plenty of centenarians and over-one-hundred-year-olds living on the islands of Okinawa. But not only that, heart disease, cancer and diabetes, here, have a much lower incidence and, in general, the elderly are almost all sprightly and in perfect shape.

The reasons seem to hide in the diet. A diet made up of cereals, vegetables and fish, and very little intake of eggs, dairy products and meat, defined by the inhabitants nuchigusuiche , which literally means medicine for life, would reveal the mystery of the longevity of the inhabitants of the island.

This diet was also studied by the Longevity Research Center based on the island and detailed in the book Okinawa, the island of centenarians by Bradley Willcox , Craig Willcox and Makoto Suzuki.

For years now, scientists have dedicated themselves to studying the archipelago and the people who inhabit it precisely to understand the way of life of the population and pass on the secret to others as well. As anticipated, it is not only the longevity that leaves you amazed, but also the low incidence of diseases typical of the Western world is a source of interest.

And this aspect, perhaps, does not concern only the diet, but precisely the way of life. People here live in a relaxed way, meditation is widely practiced, as well as walks by the sea at sunset are an established habit. The inhabitants of the islands live according to the rhythms of nature, they do not get stressed and are never in a hurry. Their motto? Always look on the bright side of things.

For the Japanese, everyone has an " ikigai ", which a French philosopher would translate as raison d ' être ("reason for being").

The ikigai is hidden within you and requires patient exploration to reach the deepest part of our being and find it.

According to the natives of Okinawa, the island with the highest longevity rate in the world, ikigai is the reason we wake up in the morning.

One of the surprising things about the Japanese is how people live their lives even after retirement. Indeed, a large number of Japanese never "retire" from active life, they continue to work on what they like, as long as their health allows.

Some longevity studies suggest that having clear ikigai is just as important as a healthy Japanese diet.

The concept we are about to explore is particularly rooted in Okinawa, one of the so-called "blue zones", the places in the world where people live the longest.

There are more people over 100 years old per 100,000 inhabitants on this island than in any other region on the planet. There are many centenarians with a level of vitality and a state of health that would be unthinkable in the elderly of other latitudes.

In addition to living many more years than the rest of the world population:

They have fewer chronic diseases (cancer or heart disease) and fewer inflammatory conditions

They have fewer free radicals in the blood (responsible for cellular aging) thanks to the culture of tea and light food

Cases of dementia have a significantly lower rate than the world population average and it has been seen that menopause in women occurs at a much older age

In general, men and women maintain a high level of sex hormones into old age

The researchers point out that an important part of Okinawans' health and longevity is due to their " ikigai attitude " to life, which gives each day a profound meaning.

North of the island of Okinawa, there is a population known as "the village of the centenarians". Ogimi has the honor of being the city with the highest longevity index in the world.

But what is their "secret"?

Some observations and studies on their lifestyle have shown that:

- 100% of the respondents have an orchard
- Each one belongs to a neighborhood association where they feel loved as if they belonged to a family
- They celebrate a lot, even the little things. Music, song and dance are an essential part of their day
- They have an important mission in life, or even several. They own an ikigai , but they don't take it very seriously either. There is always some relaxation and fun in what they do
- They are very proud of their local traditions and culture
- They show passion for everything they do, no matter how important it may be

- The yui-maru , which could be translated as "spirit of mutual cooperation", is engraved in their hearts. They help themselves not only in agricultural work, but also in building a house or volunteering in public works

- They are always busy, but with different tasks that allow them to relax

To live longer, it is definitely necessary to live better, to be happier.

Here are guidelines, passages, tips inspired by Japanese centenarians.

1. ALWAYS KEEP ACTIVE, NEVER STOP

Whoever abandons the things he loves loses the meaning of his life, he loses the right path. Therefore, even after finishing the "official" working life, it is important to continue to do things of value, to provide beauty or usefulness to others, to help and shape our little world.

2. TAKE LIFE WITH CALM

As the old saying goes: "Whoever goes slowly, goes healthy and far". When we leave behind non-priority things and thoughts, time and life acquire a new meaning.

3. DO NOT EAT EXAGGERATELY

To have a long life, even in food we must apply the saying " less is more ". The Japanese do not eat excessively, but adequately.

Indeed, it is popular to get up from the table while still leaving "some room" in the stomach. This will allow you to be less weighted, more productive and more active.

4. SURROUND YOURSELF WITH GOOD FRIENDS

They are a good remedy for avoiding worries. Have a good chat, tell and listen to anecdotes that lighten your existence, ask for advice, have fun together, share, dream ... In short, live.

5. STAY IN SHAPE

You must be like Water that moves, flows fresh and does not stagnate. Likewise, your body needs a little daily maintenance so that it can last for many years. In addition, exercise secretes the hormones of happiness.

6. SMILE

A positive attitude relaxes the person and spreads positive energy to those around you. It's okay to sometimes make bad choices, but don't forget the privilege of being here and now in this world full of possibilities.

7. RECONNECT WITH NATURE

We must regularly return to reconnect with nature to charge the batteries of the soul. Although most humans live in cities, we are made to merge with nature.

8. SAY THANK YOU

To nature that provides you with air and food, to your life

companions, to everything that brightens your day and makes you feel happy to be alive. Take a moment of the day to say thank you and you will increase your flow of happiness.

9. FOLLOW YOUR IKIGAI

Inside you there is a passion, a unique talent that gives meaning to your days and pushes you to give your best to the end.

If you haven't found it yet, your next mission will be to find it

10. LIVE IN THE MOMENT

Stop complaining about the past and fearing the future.

All you have is today. Make the most of it and maybe others can benefit from you and what you have to offer!

CHAPTER 11

WHAT IS THE HARA HABA BU

Well, who would not like to blow out the 100 candles while remaining in perfect health. According to science it is possible. In fact, the maximum limit inherent in our DNA would allow us to reach the age of 120 while remaining healthy. What many are asking, and to which many cannot give a certain answer, is whether there is a secret to longevity.

It happens, in fact, that even those who lead a healthy life could suddenly be struck down by an illness. In short, unfortunately, there is no way to behave that guarantees longevity.

However, there are habits that everyone can decide to adopt to increase the likelihood of living longer.

So let's see what hara is hachi bu , the secret of the Japanese to live long and in good health.

It is well known, in fact, that Japan is the country with the highest number of centenarians in the world. It would even be 20 for every 100,000 inhabitants.

The secret of longevity in Japan lies in the fact that many respect the hara rule hachi bu . According to this Confucian rule, you must eat until you are 80% full. Therefore, a 20% appetite must always remain and one must never get up from the table completely sated. Indeed, the Japanese believe that staying at the table, after having satisfied 4/5 of one's appetite, makes it easy to give in to the temptation to continue eating out of mere gluttony.

In other words, not satisfying our appetite for that 20% is the secret of a long life.

Who lives longer

Scientific studies have also shown that vegetarians live longer than those who eat meat. People who remain mentally and physically active and engaged into old age are also longer-lived.

We have thus revealed what hara is hachi bu , the secret of the Japanese to live long and in good health.

Hara hachi bun me (腹 八分 目) is a Confucian principle-

the beginning of the 21st century, Okinawans in Japan have continued to practice hara hachi bu . They consume 1,800 to 1,900 kilo-calories per day. The typical body mass index (BMI) of their seniors is around 18 to 22, compared to a typical BMI of 26 or 27 for adults over 60 in the United States. Okinawa has the highest percentage of centenarians in the world, around 50 per 100,000 people.

Authors Bradley and Craig Wilcox and Makoto Suzuki believe it hara hachi can act as a form of calorie restriction, thus extending life expectancy . This is thought to be due to the delay in stomach stretch receptors that help signal satiety. The result of not practicing hara hachi bu is a constant stretching of the stomach which in turn increases the amount of food needed to feel full.

Confucian teaching , dating back to the 5th century BC, has a similar saying to the Japanese one found in Traditional Chinese Medicine: " Chifan Qi fēn bǎo San fēn ji "(吃饭七分 饱,三分饥," eat only until you are 70 percent full. ") Japan has been heavily influenced by Chinese culture.

The principle also appears in Ayurvedic medicine, dating back to the 4th century BC , where "you should fill a third of the stomach with liquid, another third with food and leave the rest empty".

In the zen book "The Three Pillars of Zen" , the author quotes Hakuun Yasutani in his lecture for zazen beginners as he tells his students about the book Zazen Yojinki (Precautions to Observe in Zazen), written around 1300, which advises practitioners to eat about two-thirds of their capacity.

" Hara Hachi Bu “, eat until you are 80% full, this is the secret of the longevity of the citizens of the Rising Sun. They are studying them to find out if this is the key to a long and healthy life. Okinawa in Japan is home to the people who have the longest life expectancy in the world. Reaching the century of life is not the exception, but the norm. Hara Hachi Bu The Japanese secret

Under scrutiny by a flood of scientists

There are countless scholars and scientists who have dealt with this phenomenon. Here the population not only lives for many years, but does so with a high degree of health. They are overwhelmingly self-sufficient centenarians. Obviously, living long and well is the desire of many of us, for this reason on the island of Okinawa the teams of scholars take turns to discover what is the secret of this peaceful survival.

Hara Hachi Bu

It is a dietary lifestyle that can roughly translate into a full belly up to 80%. Nutritionists say this traditional health principle can be learned. Everyone can learn how to use it. Filling your stomach completely makes digestion difficult and takes time to dispose of what we have ingested. A full belly accelerates the cell oxidation processes that lead to faster aging of the body.

A very light regime

Residents of the island eat without ever reaching complete satiety. Their diet is less than 2000 calories per day, compared to 2200-2500 calories recommended for Europeans and Americans. A reduction of more than 20% of the food consumed. If the stomach is not completely full, the extra space makes digestion easier. The whole process happens more quickly, breaking down food appropriately. If, on the other hand, we eat until we are full, we make digestion more complex. The stomach stretches and the slowing down leads to sleepiness and some problems to our health.

Ideal for the "bellyless"

Those who practice the " Hara Hachi Bu "can count on some benefits. The first is aesthetic, by keeping the stomach not too full you get a wasp waistline. Digestion is never problematic, but fast. It manages to fight obesity, metabolic disorders and cancels reflux problems. The acidity with this type of regimen is lowered and the gastrointestinal functions also benefit from it. Okinavans have a low level of free radicals, which is why they have a lower risk of cardiovascular disease, cancer and other diseases related to old age.

How to follow the Hara Hachi Bu

1) Restore muscle memory - The stomach is used to large meals to let him know the new smaller amount of food ingested it will need to be trained. It takes about a week for the stomach to stop asking for more food . After about twenty meals he will get used to it.

2) Avoid going beyond the hunger signal - Eating right means leaving the table with a slight feeling of hunger. Without getting to excesses that are more like fasting. Eating less doesn't mean starving or eating things that aren't palatable. Few but good, also selected for quality, now that you eat less you can focus on better foods.

3) Eating slowly - Greed makes you overeat, slowing the pace of chewing and swallowing will make you feel satisfied and full.

4) Vegetables always come first - Eat balanced but never give up on antioxidants, they are the ones that will keep you young and healthy. Add proteins and carbohydrates in the right proportions, do

not deny yourself anything but do it in small quantities, varying your diet a lot, but always with fresh vegetables.

5) Also help with your eyes - Avoid large plates, if you serve them in smaller plates you will give the feeling of having eaten enough without having to do an encore. The stomach will soon get used to the new dimensions and it will be much easier to do the Hara Hachi Bu . Hara Hachi Bu The Japanese secret.

This ancient Confucian mantra (loosely translated means "eat until eight parts (out of ten) full), is repeated at the beginning of a meal. The purpose is to finish the meal with 80% satiety. This is the guiding principle of longevity. of the citizens of Okinawa in Japan, where the longest-lived people in the world live. Hara Hachi Bu is a lifestyle that regulates the food sphere, which finds its meaning in a food control. Eat slowly and just enough without overdoing it. An unbalanced diet slows down digestion and accelerates the processes of oxidative stress that lead to faster aging of the body.

CHAPTER 12
THE OKINAWAN DIET

Have you ever heard of ishokudoghen ? In Japanese it means "food is a medicine" and it is the philosophy with which the Japanese approach food. The use of a specific type of cooking, the choice of one food instead of another, the timing for consuming meals: everything is ishokudoghen for them. This popular belief probably harks back to the historical period in which there was not an abundance of food in Japan and supplies were in short supply. For this, the solution was to cover a sense of poverty with a philosophy of life, in which food is better than rationed.

The diet that the inhabitants of the Okinawa archipelago refer to is very simple and is strongly influenced by Taiwanese and Chinese influences: very few carbohydrates, lots of fish (strictly fresh), vegetables and fruit. Above all, fish is consumed in triple quantities compared to what is eaten on average in Japan.

Recent studies have shown that the population of these islands tends to be thin and consumes 10% fewer calories than the rest of Japan and even 40% fewer than the West. A strong point of this diet is the type of cooking of food: absolutely no to frying and grilling that generate carcinogenic compounds; steaming is better, but boiled or sautéed food is just fine too.

How does it work

A daily menu includes three main meals and low calorie snacks, such as fresh fruit and vegetables, are allowed. The Okinawan diet is based on a very low calorie content of around 1,200 calories per day, which is 20% less than other diets. A mantra of this diet is that you should never feel full. Better to stop when you are not full and focus your energies on something else.

The presence of green, yellow and orange vegetables allows the body to introduce a high concentration of antioxidants. These foods are rich in antioxidant vitamins that help fight premature aging.

The limitation of fats and sugars, on the other hand, leads to a lowering of the risk of stroke and heart disease: in the Okinawan diet, fats are practically zero.

Foods

The Okinawa archipelago is located in the stretch of sea between Japan and Taiwan. The inhabitants can therefore enjoy a lot of fresh fish, which is practically a constant on the tables of local families. Meat and dairy products are consumed very rarely and a diet that is mainly based on food of vegetable origin is preferred: sweet potatoes or rice (not so much, since not much is grown on these islands) are the primary source of carbohydrates; vitamins and mineral salts are taken thanks to the many vegetables (mostly raw) and fruit.

The proteins, on the other hand, come from legumes (especially soybeans) and from tofu, a food that unites the whole of the East. In Okinawa then, food is flavored not with salt but with spices and in particular with curry, which has anti-aging properties. Alcohol , on the other hand, is practically banned from the table.

The benefits

The Okinawa archipelago is part of the so-called "Blue Zone", which is an area where life expectancy is significantly higher than that of any other country. The average life span is 81.2 years and the centenarians are about 20% of the population. Yes, you got it right, 20%. But the centenarians here are in excellent health, they often continue to work and it is easy to meet them while jogging. In fact, alongside a healthy diet, physical exercise is essential to keep fit.

Japan itself is the longest-lived nation with twenty centenarians for every hundred thousand inhabitants, however the Okinawa archipelago with this data is also an exception for the Japanese themselves. Here it was noted that cardiovascular diseases are reduced by 80% compared to the United States, cancers are 40% less.

In addition, in the United States and Japan the risk of developing senile dementia becomes quite high from the age of eighty, while in Okinawa the increase is much more contained.

The Okinawan diet is very complete and varied. The only

contraindication is if it affects the quality of the food. For example, if the soy consumed was GMO, it could be a problem, or if the catch came from a polluted sea, would alter the caloric and beneficial intake of the food .

Foods that are consumed with a lot of limitation:

Meat: Although the Okinawan diet allows for the consumption of meat (pork is eaten for example), it does so in small quantities especially during holidays or special occasions. In the rest of the time the inhabitants generally consume a mainly vegetable diet.

Cereals: especially those with gluten should be avoided as this protein consumed in excess can cause digestive problems, inflammation, difficulty in absorbing nutrients and allergic reactions. Steamed brown rice is consumed more frequently (although much less than in the rest of Japan) and quinoa.

Dairy: Okinawans and most Asian cultures consume very little milk. When you eat milk or dairy products you prefer raw, as pasteurization in fact causes them to lose useful substances. The alternatives that can be used are coconut milk or almond milk.

After having told you what the philosophy of the Okinawan diet is and now the menu with its benefits and cons (such as excessive consumption of soy could reduce testosterone in men and promote polycystic ovary syndrome in women). However, the benefits are many, from weight loss to an increase in average life. It is no coincidence that it is also called the Okinawan centenarian diet. Here is the sample Okinawa menu!

MONDAY

Breakfast: 3 slices of sunflower seed bread, an apple, 1 soy yogurt, a cup of green tea.

Lunch: 70 g of brown rice dressed with mushrooms, cherry tomatoes, corn, salad and spinach, a slice of rye bread, a cup of green tea.

Dinner: omelette with spinach, shrimp topped with lemon, a pear, a cup of green tea.

TUESDAY

Breakfast: muesli with dried fruit, a cup of rice milk, a kiwi, a cup of green tea

Lunch: Mixed salad with cucumbers and tomatoes, smoked salmon with a slice of sunflower seed bread, two mandarins, a cup of green tea.

Dinner: Roast pork with soybeans and pineapple, mixed salad, a pear, a cup of green tea.

WEDNESDAY

Breakfast: 2 rye biscuits, a cup of green tea, an orange, a low-fat soy yogurt.

Lunch: Grilled salmon steak with sesame seeds, accompanied by mixed grilled vegetables, four slices of pineapple, a cup of green tea.

Dinner: mixed vegetable soup with 70 g of brown rice, grilled eggplant with a slice of rye bread, a kiwi, a cup of green tea.

THURSDAY

Breakfast: a smoothie with seasonal fruit, two slices of wholemeal bread, a cup of green tea

Lunch: 70g brown rice with hot peppers, a slice of rye bread, a soy milk yogurt, a cup of green tea

Dinner: Salad with spinach and curried shrimp, grilled cod, a cup of green tea.

FRIDAY

Breakfast: a cup of green tea, a kiwi, a cup of soy milk with two wheat germ cookies.

Lunch: Wholegrain noodles in a pan with curry, zucchini and shrimp, a cup of green tea, four slices of pineapple.

Dinner: a tuna steak with caraway seeds and soy germ, a slice of rye bread, a cup of green tea.

CHAPTER 13
THE TAI CHI

If we were to put some ally of longevity at the forefront, we would choose:> sleep; > meditation; > conscious breathing and chewing; > tai chi chuan.

In particular, the latter is mentioned among the most useful disciplines for the over 50s (but also 60 and 70 and 80, 90 here I have never seen it personally) and in fact science only by about ten years recognizes its benefits, not because they were not there, but because, as you can imagine, if with a drug I can isolate the effects in the laboratory and then study the individual variables, how do I behave with something that does not act locally but has a effect on the whole organism, a widespread and regenerating influence?

If then in yoga we have the nadis and chakras, in the Taoist physiology we have the five centers, the eight psychic channels and the twelve meridians that run through the surface of the body and cannot reveal themselves as Physical Methods: In Taoist terms, it could be said that, as a macro-movement, in the very adult stage, the yang gives way to an energy that moves towards recollection. The tai chi allows these two energies to work at the level of the "microcosm", that is, according to the movements that inhabit the body, which are always present, complementary, dialoguing. Legend has it that the idea of tai chi chuan was an immortal Taoist named Chang San-feng. Not that with practice you become a Taoist, but .... The benefits of tai chi for the elderly The movements of tai chi are divided into parades, trunk rotations, hand gestures to be performed with concentrated mind and conscious breathing. the movements evoke martial applications. Pushing forward, pulling back, pushing, separating your hands, simulating shoulder strikes, punches, kicks, and steps in various directions.The gentle movement and determination in wanting to learn the sequence can prove to be very useful ingredients for those who in this civilization are often considered "waste", as "no longer productive." of over-sixties who perfectly know sequences, applications, shapes with weapons. There are also many in the West and it is wonderful to see them at work.

Tai chi offers numerous benefits to the elderly, which is why On a practical level, discipline, practiced regularly, lowers blood pressure, slows the respiratory rate and generates a general condition of relaxation. joints and mood, promptness and lightness of mind. Furthermore, practicing with others is a real form of sharing, one does not feel isolated, the moments of aggregation multiply. Finally, the body is more balanced and this greatly reduces the risk of falls and possible bone breaks, such as those affecting the femur.When an elderly person falls there can be other consequences related to fear (which acts on the kidneys) such as heart attacks , heart attacks, increased episodes of high blood pressure. With age, bones become brittle, blood vessels become clogged, and the body loses flexibility. With tai chi one comes to gently meet these phenomena related to being alive for a long time. The practice also has a powerful effect on menopause and related disorders. Also find out who the master of tai chi chuan is and what he does Tai chi, science, aging Recent research by the department of neuropsychiatry at the China Medical University Hospital in Thaichung has been carried out on the influence that the practice has on particular stem cells, the CD34 +, involved in the fundamental processes of cell self-renewal, differentiation and proliferation. The study group, under the guidance of Shinn-Zong Lin, recruited a group of volunteers under 25, subsequently randomly divided into three groups, who have been asked to practice Tai chi, brisk walking or not do any physical exercise. The study lasted a year and the rejuvenation results were incredibly higher for the first group devoted to the study of Chinese energy gymnastics. The study was published and is added to recent research carried out in the United States, United Kingdom, Australia and Korea. At present, the research already carried out has shown that tai chi positively affects heart failure, on patients with mild or moderate heart disease. arkinson, in cases of fibromyalgia and arthrosis, on type 2 diabetes and osteoporosis.

Tai Chi Chuan (Taijiquan) is an ancient Chinese "internal" or soft martial art, often practiced for the benefits it guarantees to health and spirit; it is not competitive and it is light; generally follows a slow pace. Contrary to the all-Western concept of "if you don't suffer you get nothing", one hour of Tai Chi actually burns more calories than surfing and almost as much as you would while skiing; it is therefore a real training. But that's just one of the many benefits! By increasing body strength, flexibility and awareness, as well as mental focus, Tai Chi can also improve your health.

Warm up with proper breathing and centering. As with any martial art, it's not just about how quickly and how hard you can hit a tablet or win against an opponent. It's about having a firm hold on your mind. To clear your own, focus on your chi and increase your potential, you will need to start with proper breathing which, in turn, will allow you to center yourself.

Place your feet shoulder-width apart, not over.

Place your hand on the lower abdomen, about 5cm below the navel. Push lightly.

Slowly inhale and exhale through the nose by exercising this area of the abdomen. If you don't feel any movement in this area, push a little more with your hand.

Focus on all parts of your body individually. After doing the abdominal breathing, start relaxing each part of your body one at a time. Start with the feet and finish with the scalp. If you feel like it, also work with the smallest parts, such as nails. You will find that you are in tension without realizing it.

If you start to wobble, that's actually a good sign! It means that you are relaxing and that your body is not in tension to balance itself. If this happens, you can readjust your feet slightly or shift your focus on your balance until you find yourself stable again.

Rooted. One of the concepts of Tai Chi is grounding. It's pretty self-explanatory: imagine you have roots sticking out from under your feet. Be part of the ground, never lose balance, focus or center. Your limbs sway like branches in the wind, without hesitation out of fear or apprehension. Here: so you are well rooted.

This does not mean that you or your legs are stiff, quite the opposite. Try to imagine that you have roots underneath you, as part of you, that allow you some freedom of movement so that you can't fall, can't slip, and can always be a part of the natural world.

Think about your facility. In Tai Chi, your postures can take many forms. Generally each style favors a specific one. Here is a summary of the basic ones:

Small structure. This style (usually for the Wu or Hao versions) is usually very restrained. The movements are more limited and there is less extension in general. One focuses on the internal energy to form the correct transitions and movements.

Great facility. This style (Chen and Yang) involves high and low stances, more drastic postures and swinging arms. Emphasize correct body positioning and alignment in order to develop energy.

There is also an intermediate style between the previous two.

Practice with different styles. Since each type of Tai Chi is good for you, it is more important to do any one than to worry about which style is best for you. But once you are immersed in this world, you may want to experiment. Here is a brief summary:

The Chen style mixes the rhythms, going from very slow to explosive. It can be difficult for beginners.

Yang style is the most popular. It has a constant rhythm and, as mentioned before, uses very large movements. It probably matches what you think of Tai Chi.

In the Wu style, the movements are almost microscopic. The movements are very slow and thoughtful.

The Hao style is not very popular. You will probably not be able to find a teacher to practice it.

Learn the moves by understanding their philosophy and its creators. To understand the nature of Tai Chi Chuan (which means "fist of the supreme movement"), we must contextualize it in its culture of origin. This means that we have to look closely at Chinese culture and, in particular, the spiritual tradition of Taoism, in which Tai Chi Chuan bases the prop re roots and their own nourishment.

Now, what you need to know about Taoism and those who call themselves Taoists is that this philosophy of thought is intrinsically linked to nature. Not only that outside of us, but also that of our interiority. In fact, one of the key principles of Taoism comes from the Tao Teh Ching, written by the sage Lao Tzu. This principle is called Tzu Jan or Ziran in pinyin and indicates being oneself or embodying one's nature. So, in addition to the benefits that the organism derives from it and the alleviation of stress, Tai Chi Chuan is also a means to rediscover one's inner inner self.

It is much more than a move. It is not a question of simply extending your arms out in front of you ... Not at all. For each moment there is a particular purpose, flow and, for some, an application in combat.

Try the whip move. Here we describe just a few of the many, but a move that is seen quite often is that of the single whip. It is the figure where every point of the arms and upper torso is part of a whip - these body parts could explode with force at any moment, becoming the end of the whip. It doesn't seem that easy said that!

For this move, one hand generally remains in the "beak" position. As you can intuitively understand, it looks like some kind of bird's beak. The four fingers should lightly touch the thumb and the palm of the hand should be facing down. As for the arms, each style of Tai Chi is slightly different, but they are generally held at shoulder height and unfold like loose wings.

The arms should move in opposite ways: one should be moving fast and in different planes, while the other should be slow and cautious, never limp and weak.

The name of this move has a sweet sound, but it's actually combat. Think about it: your weight and arm position change all the time. And when all of your weight is on one leg, the other is free to kick. Everything has a meaning!

Practice the "pouring". It's something you can even queue up in the mail! Simply stand with your feet on the floor, parallel, shoulder-width apart. Then you shift your weight onto one leg and hold it; after a few inhalers and exhalations, slowly transfer your center of gravity to the other leg and stay still. Repeat for a few minutes, clearing your mind and becoming aware of your balance.

Make circles with your arms. At first do it with your fingers only, then move on to the wrists, forearms and finally to the whole shoulder. Try to constantly maintain perfect balance.

Make circles with your feet too! Sit down and work from the fingers to the thighs, bending the knees when necessary. Make sure you go both clockwise and counterclockwise.

Master the "snake crawling down" move. Once again it must be specified that this move is slightly different for each style of Tai Chi, even if the general sense is common: to go from a standing position to a deep lunge (hamstring) in the most gentle way possible.

Once this movement is done, test your balance with your arms. Move them on different planes and at different speeds. Can you hold this position?

Switch from a short to a long form. As with most beginners, you will probably stick to the first one. There are 13 to 40 moves and it generally lasts 5-20 minutes. After that, you will probably want to do more, and at that point pr overai the long type! This is 80 or more moves that take more than an hour. You will benefit from it in terms of stress!

Choose a Tai Chi style that suits your needs and interests. There are hundreds of them, but each has its own goal in terms of health or martial arts. You will have to make a decision as to what you want to achieve from the Tai Chi experience. The six most popular styles, which come from as many families, are the Chen, Yang, Wu, Sun, Wu-Hao and Fa styles. The Yang style is the most popular for health reasons, while the Chen style is best known as the art of self defence. Whatever style it is, practice and remember that they all share the same basic philosophy.

There are over 100 Tai Chi movements and positions to learn, often named after animals or related to nature.

The common substrate among all forms of Tai Chi is the concentration on the breath coordinated with the rhythmic movement, and the final goal of achieving inner calm by focusing on the present.

Assess your eligibility. Anyone can do Tai Chi, as long as they choose the lightest ways to practice it. The reason is that Tai Chi emphasizes technique and not strength, giving everyone the opportunity to master the art regardless of strength or age. The workout is low impact and is therefore ideal for most people. If in doubt, talk to your doctor.

People who have joint, spine or heart problems or fractures and pregnant women should discuss it with their doctor.

Find an experienced and suitable instructor for you. There are no degrees or skills to teach Tai Chi, and the key factor is the compatibility of your learning with the teaching style. While there are some helpful study guides, it's simply impossible to learn from a book or video. A DVD cannot correct your form, and everyone needs guidance as a beginner. Furthermore, the social support guaranteed by the attendance of the lessons is priceless. Places to find a Tai Chi instructor include local and city hall-run clubs and gyms, especially those that specialize in teaching martial arts. Online you will find numerous resources for your research. Factors for choosing an instructor include:

There is no universal (or widely used) accreditation system for Tai Chi instructors.. A teacher without the ability to answer questions and give students personalized directions is not acceptable, so you may want to trust your instincts and keep searching until you get the spark with the right one.

If you have just started practicing Tai Chi, it is perfectly acceptable to learn from an advanced level student.

An important factor to consider is any physical ailments you have, which will require special attention. If they include illnesses such as arthritis or multiple sclerosis, it is essential to opt for an instructor who has experience in making changes for people who suffer from the same condition as you.

Choosing an instructor who teaches in a gym an hour away from your home is the easiest way to relegate Tai Chi to the New Year's Resolution Corner, year after year. Make sure you find classes somewhere close and easily accessible.

Pay for a course you can afford. Going to a fancy gym and wearing a certain uniform doesn't make much sense if you don't learn anything. The more traditional lessons are held outdoors and are informal when compared, for example, to those of the taekwondo school.

Choose a style of education. Whether your Tai Chi teacher is a busy suburban housewife or an elderly white-bearded Chinese man, opt for a learning style that suits you. As experienced as the instructor is, if you fail to understand it you will not gain anything from the experience and it will be difficult to practice. Make sure you select a master who has the same goals as you (in terms of health, self-defense, etc.). To understand what you're up against, attend a class before signing up. Teachers who refuse to give a trial lesson are hiding something. All arrogant instructors who insist on being called "grandmaster" or some other similarly exaggerated title are not worth the trouble. A true Tai Chi master will tell you that he is still learning to master the art, even after so many years.

Keep in mind that Tai Chi distances itself from competition. You don't go to class to fight the teacher or your classmates. Go to class to honor and extend the teacher's work and to learn.

Practice. According to anecdotes about a Tai Chi master, the renowned Chen Fake, he practiced the forms more than 30 times a day. While you certainly don't have to go this extreme, training once a day is essential. Practicing twice a week is the bare minimum to learn more effectively and feel a tangible benefit. When you train, focus on what you remember. Don't blame yourself if you have a memory lapse, improve what you can work on. While remembering only one position, getting up and holding it will do you good.

Develop a routine that is easy to remember and allows you to make a pleasant association between practicing Tai Chi and how you feel about your day in general.

What you gain from practicing Tai Chi is largely determined by how and how much you practice. To get the most out of your training, you need to be consistent. Set aside time for yourself every day (15 minutes will suffice). Then, every day, take your time to heal your body and clear your mind through practice. The reward will be worth all the effort.

You can train indoors or outdoors, with friends or alone. Find the one that suits you best and Tai Chi will become a real pleasure.

Make a commitment to practice for a minimum of 12 weeks. You need at least three months of training before you notice any benefits. At this point, what you have gained will be evident and will now represent a part of you, but don't give up. Give yourself at least this minimum period to see improvements. And, once you reach this stage, continue to reap even greater and more lasting benefits, along with a tremendous increase in your abilities.

Remove distractions from the practice area. During the Tai Chi session, you will need to put aside everything that is distracting you and concentrate. Deep breathing and relaxation will help you.

Take it easy. Keeping the body tense is the best way to ensure that you don't get any benefit from Tai Chi. However, relaxing doesn't mean you have to sprawl on the floor. Maintain correct positions without excess tension. Classical Tai Chi literature describes how to hold the posture as if "a thread placed on your head made you stretch upward".

Breathe. The secrets of Tai Chi's health benefits depend, in part, on deep abdominal breathing. Most styles teach breathing through the diaphragm: inhale by expanding the abdominal area (not the chest) and exhale by contracting the abdominal muscles. The inhalation occurs only through the nose, while the exhalation through the mouth, with the tongue that should touch the roof of the mouth, stimulating the salivation function.

Live the moment. Develop Tai Chi mental discipline to live in the moment, instead of focusing on anxiety.

Practice in stressful situations. Once you get better at Tai Chi, make it a part of your daily life to reduce stress. Practice the concepts of Tai Chi in situations of greater tension, such as traffic and high-intensity work meetings, to relieve stress and to restore inner calm and balance.

As a form of meditation, Tai Chi can help you understand yourself better and therefore have a more efficient relationship with others. So when a stressful situation arises, learning Tai Chi will help you be assertive and respectful of others, as well as live in the present and deal with the situations in front of you with extreme calm. Tai Chi gives the opportunity to blend the opposing forces of yin and yang, one's inner self and the world, with the aim of achieving a natural balance for physical and spiritual well-being. This balance is represented by the Tai Chi symbol.

Expand your repertoire. Exploring the various forms and styles after reaching a basic level of mastery is always very helpful in improving your general knowledge of Tai Chi. The iconic practice of Tai Chi involves forms with the hands and slow movements performed in groups or alone. But Tai Chi includes a broad g amma of forms that can restore your health and self-defense skills. Most instructors proceed to such forms only after acquiring demonstrable proficiency in the basic forms of the hand style.

Learn about weapon shapes. Almost all styles of Tai Chi, including those that ignore martial intent, have forms practiced with weapons. They can range from simple sticks to swords, passing through the esoteric Chinese weapons.

Find out about the partner's work. If the practice of the forms represents the individualized workout of Tai Chi, the tui shou ("push the hands") is the couple exercise. While it may ultimately lead to free training, tui shou is practically an exercise designed to develop the sensitivity and acquisition of Tai Chi skills in a cooperative way. In principle, the learning of tui shou is built regularly; one moves from the patterns of fixed positions with one hand and ends with a pattern of movement with both hands, sometimes varying the height and speed.

Read many books on Tai Chi and do it thoroughly. Lessons help you learn, but the significance, philosophical core, and history of Tai Chi takes some commitment and is best dealt with by reading and learning at your own pace. This is an important part of studying Tai Chi, because it gives you the opportunity to gain a deeper understanding of how martial art benefits you mentally and physically and makes it possible to discover new ideas about enriching your training experience. Other people who are learning martial art can pass on other information to you and you may want to apply some of their ideas to see if they are right for you.

Don't be afraid to ask the instructor questions about the solitary learning part, such as what to read and questions about what you have read. Thus, you will further expand your understanding.

Read the "Tao Te Ching" and "I Ching" to find out more, and also look for books that offer interpretations of them. These books deal with the concept of "who" and how to control it in order to feel better overall.

Think of moving your body as if it were a single unit, not a set of sections. To push your hands forward, push with your legs and move your entire torso forward instead of just moving your arms. Traditionally, this is described as the movement that occurs from your "dan tien", the center of the body, located just below the navel. Moving your whole body in an integrated way is the source of your "inner power" (in the jin) in applying Tai Chi to self defense.

Move slowly and at an even pace. Remember that you are not

only exercising your body, you are also training your energy, which is contained in your body.

Warnings

Tai Chi is a martial art and, originally, its ultimate goal was combat. Don't think it's just "Chinese exercise", otherwise you may offend traditional practitioners. As if this were not enough, this is often considered a symptom of ignorance.

Keep your knees from going over the tip of your toes or collapsing inward. This is a very common beginner mistake when trying to relax and stay "grounded" on the floor, but doing so can cause serious knee injuries.

CHAPTER 14

UKEIRERU : THE JAPANESE ART OF ACCEPTANCE

The Japanese word Ukeireru means acceptance. Or rather, there are 4 words in Japanese that have this meaning (Ukeireru , Uketomeru , Toriireru and Ukenagasu) but each of them has a particular nuance, the term Ukeireru can describe "when a mother makes her child accept something in a kind way, fun to imagine inside ".

We had already seen what the principles of Ichigo were Ichie , the philosophy of carpe diem, is to take advantage of every moment, but how can we practice the acceptance of Ukeireru in our daily life?

Acceptance understood by Ukeireru , is an acceptance towards what we are and those around us (family, friends, colleagues ...), it is an acceptance of reality to broaden the limiting perspective that we sometimes have of us and of our life.

By accepting others, one is also able to understand them more, to understand their point of view, which could be totally different from ours, but with the desire to understand it and not judge it. And it is when you arrive at this acceptance that you are able to change the situation by eliminating the stress that created it.

Ukeireru is therefore acceptance as a lifestyle aimed at change.

The first step to create this lifestyle aimed at acceptance, is therefore to become aware of what is happening around us and accept it as it is. Only once you have taken this step, you can move on to the second: use your imagination and your ideas to create well-being, not only for you but also for those around you.

In doing so, the change is not seen as something negative but as something natural that happens, which we cannot stop in any way but which we can guide by accepting it and turning it in our favor. And if we feel good, we can then do things to make others feel good too.

Ukeireru is therefore a pragmatic vision, which brings out the empathic side, but it does not mean submission or yielding to others, on the contrary. Once you have the opportunity to calmly observe who and those around you, understanding their point of view, you will have more power over your emotions and you will not get carried away by anxiety, anger or stress caused by others. One way to do this is also through silence: it is only when you are committed to listening to others, and not simply hearing what they say and then responding and having your say, that you can begin to really understand them.

Then start practicing the art of accepting Ukeireru and notice all the benefits in your daily life and in your well-being.

We would all like to be happy. Through family, friendships and work, man continually seeks a way to be happy.

What is the key to happiness? There are those who try to reach it by chasing money, others give more importance to the spiritual life and still others to physical perfection. Each of us tries a different way, according to his aspirations, his desires and his needs to get closer, even slightly, to the much desired happiness.

Today we are in a historical period in which achieving this perfection seems almost impossible. Human contact has been denied to us, leisure has been suppressed and we spend the whole day dividing ourselves between work and house duties. It seems impossible to find happiness this way.

So what is the way to go?

The mental yoke of the timeline

The Westerner is never satisfied, because that is how he was raised by his parents and teachers. To have more degrees than others, a smarter-than-average partner and a job that allows them to build a house that is more beautiful than that of the neighbors.

He spends two thirds of his day with his mind projected into the future. He goes to university and thinks about the degree he will see five years later. He goes to work every day while thinking about how to improve it. He goes home every day to his family planning how to renovate the house, where to send the children to school, how to organize outings with friends.

The other third passes it on to regret the past. A lost love, a friend who betrayed him, a job where he earned more. And so he lives within a vicious circle.

With this state of mind that is anything but peaceful, he also hopes to be able to achieve happiness. So change friends, change partners, change schools, change jobs in a continuous cycle.

Attention, it is important to experience many paths in life, because without experimentation you will never be able to find the right path for you. But there is a lot of difference between a conscious search and a spasmodic obsession for the best.

Today these dynamics have reached exasperation as our lives have found themselves blocked by the pandemic. The stalemate has also blocked the frantic pursuit of happiness undertaken by many.

The Asian people, and in particular the Japanese, have a completely different concept of life and the pursuit of happiness from ours. They would be able to be happy even today.

How? Through the concept expressed by the wonderful word ukeireru . If you know a little about Japanese culture you will know that it includes words to express concepts of everyday life related to the mind and soul that the West has never contemplated in its vocabulary.

Accept to be happy thanks to ukeireru

The word ukeireru literally means acceptance. Ukeireru means being able to accept what surrounds us, which is part of our life. This means accepting the family we have, the friends we hang out with, a job that doesn't drive us crazy but gives us food, as well as accepting the negative situations we sometimes encounter.

Why is it so important to be able to accept to find true happiness? Because you avoid living with anxiety, distress, dissatisfaction, anger or frustration.

While you think about the future you think you are doing good to yourself, and this is true in theory, but if you do not do it with a calm mind and a peaceful heart you risk being overwhelmed. That is why the Japanese, before trying to improve the material aspects of their lives, accept what they have.

Travelers are familiar with the concept of acceptance. Accepting means opening up to others without prejudice, finding yourself in a new place because you have taken the wrong road, learning a ritual because it has made people live better for millennia.

Knowing how to accept is very important, and paradoxically it is also very difficult to put into practice.

Set your life according to the ukeireru principle

Now that we understand what the secret to happiness is, we are faced with a crucial question: how does it apply within everyday life?

The first step you need to take is to observe your surroundings. Observe your family and ask yourself if, despite all the flaws you can find on the worst days, it's a good or bad family. After that, analyze your work and take stock of the value it offers against the energies it requires of you. Finally, evaluate your friends, ask yourself if they help you grow or if they drag you towards the abyss.

If your family underneath makes you feel safe, if your friends help you complete you, and if work feeds you, you understand that everything is not as gray as it was before. At this point you are ready to accept. Accept everything as it is.

Furthermore, it is also important to know how to accept change. Almost all of us are reluctant to change because they lead us towards an unknown, unknown situation, which in our mind could be both positive and negative.

Knowing how to accept change is essential to live a peaceful life and remove the stress from your days.

Have you taken this step? Very well, now you can move on to the next one. Use your creativity to create your well-being.

Having eliminated the negative emotions you will find that a huge energy field has formed within you just waiting to express itself.

Now it is good to clarify that accepting does not mean giving up. Submitting to events is something negative, it is an absence of action. Acceptance, on the other hand, is action, it is a gesture that you make towards yourself to get better.

Ukeireru is a wonderful practice that incites continuous presence, the here and now .

To train it, the Japanese recommend silence, because only when you are silent can you listen to both others and yourself. So start here, listening to yourself.

CHAPTER 15
SHINRIN -YOKU

Nature is always the key, the solution to our every disturbance, the easing of every pain, the Japanese have always known this, who have made it a philosophy of life. Shinrin -yoku , in fact, is a practice born in Japan which involves immersion in a natural context; literally it means "to benefit from the atmosphere of the forest" or more simply, "bath in the forest". It is, therefore, a direct (and practical) way to detoxify from the hectic life that we are now used to living, or more correctly to undergo.

“By frequenting the forest, or the woods, and slowing down our rhythms of life, entering into harmony with nature through the senses, it is possible to invigorate the body, calm the spirit and nourish the soul. Nature is magical, we just have to find a way, or rather the time to listen to it. "

A ADVICE THAT IS ALSO A SALVATION

Nowadays we go so fast that we do not realize it, we are used to always being late, to have so many commitments, that the frenzy has become the norm. Accomplices of this increasingly widespread lifestyle are the work commitments, the thousands of external inputs, the expectations we create for ourselves, the need to earn as much as possible to keep the standard of living high, in short, there are many factors. So, how can we save ourselves from this wheel that is spinning faster and faster? And what risks making us implode in ourselves? Well easy, lower the pace, or simply try to get away from all this whirlwind. How? Going to nature! Okay, it seems easier said than done, but we need to know that if we don't, at some point, our mind will go haywire and our body will stop, facing an inevitable default. Direct contact with nature, on the other hand, can save us. As the Japanese (the wise ones) suggest, Shinrin-yoku is the solution! If we want to save ourselves, we must learn to consider Nature, and above all to take the time to immerse ourselves in it. You will then see which ones will be the same.

"Concretely, shinrin-yoku means walking in a forest without haste, letting yourself be guided by the smells and colors of nature. Observe the details of the leaves, listening to the scents of the bark, the moss, the earth. Listen to the noises around you. It is therefore an immersive experience that involves all the senses, something very similar to aromatherapy. Then, trees and plants will project us into a uterine dimension, and of total well-being. "

It is curious, however, how the concept of Shinrin-yoku was born in one of the most frenetic and aggressive societies that exist, the Japanese one, almost as if it were an instinctive reaction, a necessary maneuver of salvation, of redemption of man from the noose of modern life. Like many modern Asian societies, Japan also has a very ancient, ancestral culture, which never forgets its link with Mother Nature, although today it is the reign of prevailing technology.

WE ARE CHILDREN OF THE EARTH!

The Shinrin-yoku has its roots in a very precise concept, namely that we humans, like all other living beings, come from the Earth, and it is therefore only she who can heal us, cure us. A union between Man and Nature which, despite the distractions of modern life, remains indissoluble. We are children of the Earth, and we often forget it, or even ignore it. So let's try to find time for a walk in the woods, turn off computers and cell phones, for once, let's try to detoxify. At first it won't be easy, but then, with a little persistence, it will become a need. The need to free thoughts, ease worries, simply by walking in the woods, getting in tune with the magic of Nature.

And for those who live in the city, it is not necessary to go to a forest, a park is enough!

WHAT BENEFITS

You don't need to be an expert to reap the benefits of an "escape" into nature. Walking surrounded by greenery, in fact, relieves stress, reduces worries and helps us to reduce daily problems. Nature is a real cure-all, it is like a magical filter that regenerates and purifies us.

Shinrin -yoku is also recommended to recover from surgery or disease; it also helps those with sleep problems and helps concentration. Seeing is believing!

We were not born to live constantly in the midst of concrete and traffic, so for Western populations, bathing in the forest can be the right remedy for anxiety, stress and depression. Let's see what this 'natural therapy' born in Japan is and how it works

We are dominated by instincts, the call of a primordial essence, which often tries to take over our rationality, suddenly slipping into the repeated gestures of our daily routine.

In recent years, this internal and uncontrolled push has often been given a negative connotation, given that this word has often been associated, in the world of information, with news stories.

This is not, however, such a correct view. Instincts play a fundamental role in human life, they are essential for survival.

We think of the life instinct, which is the innate need to create, keep alive and obtain joy and pleasure, the main source of creative and positive energy in man.

Instincts are also responsible for the sensations experienced during a journey totally immersed in nature, among the scents, colors and sounds of uncontaminated nature. Perceptions shared by all those who find themselves spending time, for example, in a forest.

Our senses are enhanced, because they receive new and unprecedented stimuli, especially for a civilization used to spending most of its time in an urban or domestic environment.

It is the effect of relaxation, peace and balance that you feel when you listen to the sound of the wind in the trees, when you smell the scent of leaves wet from the rain or touch the tips of the trees.

This happens because nature manages to make the strings of our primordial instincts resonate, awakening the deep bond of man with nature.

This also explains the feeling that each of us experiences once we return from a mountain hike, which translates into the physical need to do it again.

Some speak of addiction, but it is actually a strong appeal, which leverages our most primordial self.

There are some cultures that are particularly attentive to the link between man and his origins which, despite progress, have been able to keep intact the memory and value of some traditions that are beneficial for the body and spirit of man.

We are talking about Japan, one of the most advanced nations in terms of technology and scientific research, in which ancient traditions retain their value intact even in contemporary life and culture.

Some of these traditions have been studied and deepened by science, becoming real tools of medical care. As in the case of the practice of Shinrin-yoku .

It is not easy to translate this term, it is part of those concepts of the Japanese language that have a unique meaning, to convey the idea you could use "bathroom in the forest" or use the concept of "receiving benefits from the atmosphere of the forest".

In practice, this therapy theorizes precisely the positive effects of a complete immersion in a wood or a forest. A contact with these environments which, however, must be active and free of distractions.

It is important to spend a day completely immersed in greenery, focusing on the sounds of nature, its scents, seeking contact with trees and plants, so as to allow all our senses to refine their perceptions.

We know that walking in nature brings great benefits to the body and mind. Every trekking enthusiast has experienced the well-being that a day in the woods can bring.

Science has also shown the positive effects of a lifestyle focused on constant walking for the heart, diabetes, respiratory system and for anxiety and depressive syndromes.

But in Japan something more has been done, Shinrin-yoku has in fact been the subject of a real health and social policy initiative by the Government, which over the years has encouraged and promoted the practice of the " forest bath" .

One way to encourage citizens to engage in this practice more frequently, trying to make this activity widespread among the population.

Japanese doctors often prescribe this medicine to their patients, Japan is in fact a country characterized by very high work rates and very populous and chaotic urban centers.

The bath in the woods, if practiced with a certain regularity, is able to bring great benefits to the entire immune function.

In fact, walking in nature corresponds to a natural practice of aromatherapy and sensory stimulation.

Several scientific researches have shown how this practice reduces anxiety, depression and anger, directly affecting the triggering causes of these pathologies.

In recent years, medicine has managed to demonstrate the chemical and biological mechanisms that are protagonists of the therapeutic and curative effects of baths in the forest.

These studies have found that well-being is due to the essential oils and phytocides that plants release naturally.

These fragrances, especially those emanating from conifers, known as "woody essential oils", reduce the risk of psychosocial problems related to stress.

In fact, the resins that trees produce in their natural environment, the woods, are mostly made up of terpenes. These are lipid molecules protagonists of many traditional herbal remedies.

Complex natural environments, such as woods, constitute an incredible pool of terpenes, which, based on their peculiar structure and aroma, have various positive functions on our organism.

A day of walking in a mountain or wooded environment allows us to come into contact with many varieties of these natural substances.

One of their strengths is, in fact, their great bioavailability, which allows us to absorb them through breathing, ingestion and or through skin contact.

The combined action of these varieties of terpenes acts on blood pressure, on the reduction of stress, as well as on the mechanisms of anxiety and depression, with a relaxing and calming effect.

That is why Shinrin-yoku is prescribed, not only to act on anxious and depressive states, but also in recovering from surgery or illness, improving sleep and increasing energy level.

Not only that, it would also seem able to intervene on one of the "great enemies" of young people today, victims of stress and hectic life, namely ADHD, ie the hyperactivity syndrome and the inability to concentrate.

Researcher Jose Antonio Correia , Professor of Environmental Psychology at the Autonomous University of Madrid, explains that:

“With the advent of modern society, cities have begun to represent a security against the possible aggressions of nature. We now know that this attitude is wrong and that we can even speak of deficiency disorders of nature: increased obesity, respiratory diseases, vitamin D deficiency, stress ...

The city offers us protection and comfort, but our nervous system has not fully adapted to the urban environment and therefore feels the lack of stimulation from the natural environment that has allowed the survival of our species ".

According to the researcher, we suffer from a kind of illiteracy regarding nature and we should start living in the green again to feel better.

In short, we should take a cue from Japan and try to spend more time walking in a park or in a forest.

We can let ourselves be enchanted by the wonders of nature and recover our ancestral memory and our primary instincts.

Correia himself pointed out , we can always adopt an alternative solution by taking a walk in a city park.

Even these environments can have a therapeutic action, because the natural elements typical of large woods can also be found, proportionally, in a green city area.

CHAPTER 16
KAIZEN

Kaizen method (in Japanese it means "change for the better" or "improvement") is the name of a quality management method well known and applied in the world of industry and business in general. A continuous improvement process based on concrete, simple and inexpensive actions that involve all the workers of a company and can be easily applied to daily life, meditation and the achievement of objectives.

The word Kaizen (改善) can also be translated as refinement (KAI: change - ZEN: good).

The fundamental principle of Kaizen is that not even a day must pass without having made any kind of improvement, whether at family, social or working level.

The essence of this method is that the person performs a certain task every day at the same time for one minute. One minute is a very short time, within everyone's reach.

Mindfulness Meditation for example . We can start by meditating for one minute a day for one or more weeks and then increase by one minute until we reach the goal (15 or 30 minutes a day). It is better to meditate for just one minute, rather than "not meditating for thirty minutes".

Imagine the diet. How many times have you set yourself a certain diet but don't carry it out? It is best to start by removing one food at a time. Or one bite at a time. Stopping eating chocolate, for example, when you eat a lot of it, is difficult. Try checking the portion instead. No longer a tablet, but a tablet minus a piece. For one month. And then two, and so on.

And when it comes to exercise? You cannot start exercising for an hour if you have never done any physical exertion before. At the hour, you have to get there, step by step. Starting with just one minute a day. At least for a month and then increase to two and so on.

Not to mention when you want to start saving. It is impossible not to spend more. You can start by removing an object from the cart before arriving at the checkout, or set aside one euro a day by giving up a coffee, or a newspaper etc.

Stop smoking or drinking by eliminating a cigarette or a glass of... every day for a month. And so on.

The "all at once" does not exist, it is not possible especially when we set ourselves goals. The more important they are, the more they imply change and the more we have to break them down into small daily improvements.

Often, one of the reasons why no goal is achieved is precisely because it is difficult to change one's "mindset" completely overnight. But with small daily steps, small improvements, easy for us to pursue, it is possible.

Furthermore, thanks to the Kaizen method , we can train and develop our determination.

Finally, one of the pillars of the Kaizen methodology concerns order and organization: from the home to the office desk. Each element must be useful, each object is functional to something. Cleanliness and order, this is the starting point: remove what is not needed. Obviously all this should not be understood as an exclusively physical step. Digital is also affected by this logic: the computer desktop must be organized and designed to simplify every operation.

The core of the Kaizen concept is this: you have to move towards constant improvement. There must be no sudden revolution, magic never happens. Aim for small daily improvements.

CHAPTER 17
KINTSUGI : JAPANESE ART IN WHICH GOLD HEALS WOUNDS

Kintsugi is the art of enhancing wounds. It can be considered a form of art therapy that invites you to transcend the trials you have faced by turning the lead of your existence into gold.

This sentence, taken from the book by Celine Santini, Kintsugi - The secret art of repairing life, is a metaphorical synthesis that offers a discreet introduction to the subject. A good starting point to understand the ancient Japanese technique of "repairing with gold" as a physical or artistic action and grasp its philosophical and psychological value.

Let's take a vase. The vessels break. And the first thing that comes naturally to do, after the accident or the moment of anger that caused the breakup, is to just try to go further. Maybe replacing the broken one with a new one. The kintsugi (kin : gold and tsugi : repair) instead provides another answer, a different treatment of the break and, certainly, much more demanding. That of putting the pieces back together, through a long procedure, and in a precious way, welding them with a lacquer and then decorating everything with gold dust.

Ashigaka Yoshimasa : the legend of the origin

The art of reconstructing with gold, according to the testimonies available to historians, dates back to the fifteenth century and is associated with the figure, who really existed, of the eighth shogun - military dictator at the head of the government - of the Muromachi era , Ashigaka Yoshimasa . Legend has it that, during the tea ceremony, a cup to which the shogun was very attached was broken by mistake, to the point of ordering his craftsmen to rebuild it immediately.

He did not ask for a new one, he asked to have the one he had just broken back, as it was precious, personal and unique. A common craftsman would have tried to reassemble the pieces, trying to make the joints as inconspicuous as possible. But not those in the service of the shogun. Instead they decided to recompose without trying to hide the cracks, trying instead to enhance them with resin and gold dust.

The legend does not narrate the dictator's reaction, but suggests that Ashigaka greatly appreciated the original solution proposed by his craftsmen, since since then that technique, the kintsugi , spread throughout Japan. And even today, often handed down from father to son, it continues to amaze and receive appreciation even at an international level.

Very simplistically, we could summarize kintsugi in three

techniques. The first, called Hibi , is to repair the cracks in the way described above. The second, Kake No Kintsugi Rei, involves the creation of any missing piece of the vase, making it custom-made in lacquer and gold. With the third, Jobitsugi , the craftsman uses pieces from another porcelain or an object of a different material, but usually very similar and of equal value.

But there is not only manual work behind the creation of these works of art. As the anthropologist and psychologist Gustave Le Bon would have said, "action without thought is a vain effort". And to try to understand the thought behind this technique, we can refer to the Japanese conception of Wabi - Sabi. A formula that we can translate as: wonder in front of nature and acceptance of the transience of things.

It is not just a restorative technique. Metaphorically, the fractures of the object reflect the roughness and the changes that the human being can face during his life. The repair of the broken vase along the way of the kintsugi therefore represents the possibility of repairing the wounds, recomposing without denying.

By following that same path, the person can undertake a path of healing his own inner wounds or those in relationships. And no matter how many there are: if you have the pieces and the right glue, you can rebuild, then proceeding renewed and enriched by the experience towards a new life with a form of greater perfection. Sometimes, when it comes to relationships, the central theme is that of forgiveness, as those who, for example, adopt the logic of

Kintsugi in family mediation are well aware.

The experience of forgiveness is an experience of resurrection. The love that seemed dead, finished, thrown into the dust, without hope, comes back to life, starts again, starts again.

Everything is, according to the model created centuries ago by the artisans at the shogun's court, in the capacity for resilience, understood not only as resistance. In our knowing how to transform, not hide, pain or perhaps disappointment by developing an attitude of care for ourselves and for the bonds with others.

In the last year marked by the pandemic where, in a nightmare scenario, individual wounds and social fractures have multiplied, repairing with gold has found unsurprising attention. There have been many exhibitions dedicated to this art.

Healing the wounds of the soul by transforming them into something unique and precious. Yes, because after the pain there is always a moment in which you have to "put the pieces back together". This is the teaching of Kintsugi (da, kin , oro and tsugi , repair), the Japanese art born centuries ago to repair teacups that transforms damaged and broken objects into works of art. A metaphor for a mental attitude that we should learn to live better and more at peace with ourselves and with others. For the Japanese, every “wound”, physical or emotional, is a new beginning and the resulting scars should not be hidden, but displayed with pride.

It is an ancient Japanese art that appeared apparently by chance around the 14th century when the eighth Shogun Yoshimasa , not knowing where to go to fix his favorite teacup that had fallen apart, sent it to China, sadly without outcome. Back home, skilled Japanese artisans decided to transform the cup into a precious object by filling the cracks with lacquered resin; they covered the cracks with pure gold dust. Skillful, measured and patient gestures to return the object to its life cycle, highlighting its fractures after having embellished them. History or legend, the origin of Kintsugi embodies the thought of Shinto spirituality that even objects have their own soul and should not be thrown away, but reassembled and returned to continue to be used for their function. A philosophy of respect and great creativity, which sees a life cycle in the possibility of transformation. Nothing is thrown away of what we love, to be replaced by something new, whole and perfect. Perfection is a concept that does not exist in Zen philosophy and the same whole objects coexist with their own intrinsic manufacturing differences, they are never identical, even though they are the same. Love for the irregular denotes a longing for freedom, while the perfect is static, coded and cold, as it reveals itself at first glance and leaves no room for evoking intimate differences.

Not all adversities come to harm. True, you have been injured But what matters is that you have been able to move forward, deal with the pain and rebuild your life. It took some effort, I know, and certainly the wound left some consequences, but not all of them are negative. For example, pain has made you more sensitive and more empathetic towards those who, like you, have been hurt. You have a lot to teach these people. You are reborn from your ashes and your scars are the best of evidence do not be ashamed of the scars, do not hide them. Indeed, embellish them, because they are the greatest testimony of your strength.

In the metaphor of Kintsugi , that of “embracing damage”, transforming an object embellished with golden scars into a unique and different one, we find a similar way of looking at the human being, his wounds and his traumas. Nobody is perfect, but how we manage to look at ourselves and others and what we can do with this look is important. The metaphor of Kintsugi would seem to conceive the object, in this case the person, as passive and broken, but this is not the case. On the contrary, recognizing in one's wounds, in one's pain and in one's breakdown, a lack, not concealing it or being ashamed of it, but feeling the need for attention and care, is an extremely active and vital thought, which can open to the transformation of oneself. Feeling hurt, damaged, suffering or missing, unable to maintain one's personal "wholeness" is paradoxically an act of integrity, a first way of saying ME. All this also contrasts with the pressing demands of contemporary society. The social outlook today tends more than ever to equate beauty with aesthetic perfection, job satisfaction with success, victory with overwhelming those who are not perfect or successful. It is difficult to resist this pressure, it is difficult to feel that one can make one's own weakness, one's own wound, the starting point for a path of transformation. The ideal imperative prevails to show oneself perfect, strong, performing, the urgency to bypass time and deny its value, to affirm only the now-and-now. That broken cup of Kintsugi is under the pressure of being perfect, of being denied its specific condition, of not being able to "embrace the damage". In this way each wants to be like the other, perceived as a model of perfect integrity. As in Kintsugi , however, starting a path of transformation is offered as an art, as an act to welcome one's own (and others') imperfection, weakness, wound, trauma, that is, one's inner cracks procured by life, to restore us imperfect to it. and more aware, in continuous open transformation of oneself in the life cycle.

Kintsugi offers a different interpretation of pain: by learning to respect one's own fragility and scars, one learns to heal the wounds of the soul and to become stronger people. The delicacy and patience that Kintsugi change - like psychotherapy - entails require a slow and profound transformation, which leads to reassembling the scattered pieces of oneself and one's life in a creative way. And so it also leads to freeing the mind from the pursuit of perfection, which does not exist. Indeed, it is precisely from defeats and imperfections that it is possible to perceive authentic beauty, in the same way in which the gold that embellishes the fractures gradually transforms the vase into a unique object different from what it was.

CHAPTER 18

MEDITATING TO LIVE WELL: HOW TO DO IT AND PRACTICAL ADVICE

Meditating means going inside, reading your own character and emotions. It means immersing oneself with the mind's eye towards one's essence. Doing it consistently means guaranteeing yourself many benefits and we see together only some of the many.

Calm and patience

Whoever meditates regularly gets a certain mental stillness that is brought into daily actions. The approach towards the relationships and reactions of others becomes different. We do not depend on what others think and say but we make the most of our reservoir of authentic emotions and we are able to communicate in a true and calm way. Little by little we realize that external conditions do not affect us, we can observe them but without fully "drowning" ourselves.

New eyes every day

Over the course of the days we face various experiences and various episodes or some material matters that must be carried forward step by step . Meditation teaches us to conduct them effectively and practically, but with a sense of construction that helps us keep a solid and positive mind. For example, if we thought we were not very daring or not very organized in the past, meditation allows us to re-evaluate our way of dealing with everything. We look at ourselves in a different way in the mirror and, day after day, smiling at the reflection becomes naturally and gradually possible.

Better relationship with your body

The perception we have of ourselves changes with time and goes through various phases. Meditation manages to make us accept our physical aspect and love it in the best way. we become sensitive in a different way and we begin to understand that much of our beauty lies in our thoughts and our perception. When you acquire a calm gait, your posture and the way you manage your back, your gait, and the general trim of your body also improve. Meditation also helps to support pain from physical injury or those disorders related to depression or anxiety that generate psychophysical imbalances.

Detachment

Going to understand ourselves in a profound way, we are able to create a certain detachment also with respect to the results and actions of other people. What is done outside of us assumes no greater importance than what exists in the center of our feeling. The things and the words of others hurt us less or in any case we know when to explain to the other person that we have reached a limit. Our words are weighted and we understand better what is going through us, moment by moment.

Mental openness

The moment one approaches meditation, one sees better the incessant flow of one's thoughts. Improve memory, concentration. We make decisions quickly and often these decisions turn out to be right in terms of contact with our feelings. We also find relevant creative solutions and build bridges with memories that make us feel better. Increases strength and open-mindedness, including a tendency not to give in to distractions. We also understand better the visions of others, we do not fix ourselves on our own and we become somehow "capacious".

How to approach meditation

If you have never meditated, a great way is to buy a candle. The candle lights you up from within and lets you enter the dimension of the ritual. Simply, in a moment when you are sure that you are not disturbed, turn it on and look at it, then close your eyes and surrender to your breaths, pay attention to the teaching that every breath and every inhale generates. You can put an alarm on your mobile or activate one specifically to give you a time; alternatively, you can also let the meditation go and reopen your eyes when you feel, but keeping something that creates discipline and a set time - to increase gradually if anything - helps a lot in the beginning.

If you know someone who has been practicing for a long time, you may decide to ask them to meditate together. The meditator expands their field of the heart and this routine, when created together, could facilitate your practice. It is also an excellent idea to meditate in the woods or on a meadow, preferably near a stream. Slowly find your ideal duration and focus on your breath whenever you lose focus. If in the early stages it is difficult, you can help yourself with the repetition of a mantra.

Meditating: How Many Times a Week?

Before aiming to meditate for a long time every morning and every evening, you could try to meditate two mornings a week for a time that you think is good or dedicate two evenings to this practice, before or after dinner. Sometimes the sessions will be difficult or will represent real stumbling blocks, but it remains important not to give up. Try to maintain your own center and use this initial phase to explore how complex but also pleasant it is to get to know each other better and better.

Wear comfortable clothing, choose a pillow to place over the sacrum, focus on your heartbeat and breaths. Gradually, without forcing but giving oneself discipline, meditation becomes a habit that also regulates many bodily functions and keeps your mind on and positive. You can also choose sound frequencies that help the brain and remove energy blocks. It becomes like an anchor, a protected place to grow and mature.

CHAPTER 19
CONCLUSIONS AND TIPS

Long working days, sudden upheavals and economic difficulties are just some of the many aspects that cause a continuous state of anxiety and stress.

Sometimes one may wonder what the meaning of one's life is: if it is right that all this overwhelms us to this point, if it is not the case to adopt a new philosophy that helps to face everyday life in a different way.

For Japanese culture, ikigai is a reason for being, it is the engine that allows us to get up every morning.

It is a Japanese philosophy of life, a continuous search for the meaning of life and happiness.

Ikigai can be translated by breaking the word down into iki : vita + gai: value (worth in English).

The meaning is divided into four cornerstones: mission, passion, profession and vocation and implies the constant carrying out of actions aimed at: creating, nurturing, serving, connecting and teaching.

Actions that have the ultimate goal of finding a purpose in life, a raison d'etre that everyone has hidden within himself.

Knowing the principles of ikigai can be a valid remedy for all those people, workers and non-workers, who have the constant feeling of wasting precious time and who live in a constant state of anxiety, stress and risk of burnout .

How many times do you feel you are performing a useless action, or getting lost in useless conversations or worse, living your entire existence without a specific purpose?

Feeling a constant sense of emptiness and dissatisfaction in life and at work, as we will see, is harmful to one's existence. A radical change in habits and way of thinking could be the beginning of a valid path of personal and professional growth to be undertaken.

The Japanese method of ikigai requires asking oneself four preliminary questions, the answers of which can already say a lot about themselves:

- What are you good at / do you succeed at?
- What do you love to do?
- What things you can do would people be willing to pay you for?
- What does the world need?

These four questions imply a reflection aimed at defining: passion, mission, profession and vocation.

Japanese philosophy aims to define one's life purpose. The ikigai , in other words, aims to guide the passing of everyday life making it pleasant away from: stress, anxiety and a sense of dissatisfaction.

How can ikigai change our life? According to the two scholars and authors of the book: “The Ikigai method ” Héctor García and Francesc Miralles , find your ikigai and consequently a reason for living is based on the following activities:

- identify a flow in each task or task that takes place
- proceed slowly and without worries
- follow a healthy diet and good habits in general
- cultivate friendships
- exercise daily
- smile and be optimistic
- seek a connection with nature
- develop resilience

Furthermore , ikigai bases its principles in two other important Japanese philosophies :

Wabi -Sabi

It can be translated as the imperfection of nature. That is to realize that beauty is in imperfection and should, in fact, be sought in imperfect and incomplete things.

The wabi -sabi is an invitation to appreciate and recognize the beauty in imperfection. A first step to take towards personal growth.

Ichi-Go Ichi-E

It is an effort that each of us should make: focus on the present and fully live every moment offered by life. It is therefore, the achievement of the awareness that each moment is unique and will not return.

The philosophy in question, in many respects, recalls the Latin aphorism Carpe diem (seize the day), that is, the invitation to take care and enjoy every single moment.

In summary, nature is imperfection, time is fleeting. Ikigai , a philosophy that aims to find the meaning of life , is based on these considerations .

There is no definite method or magic recipe for finding your ikigai , however Wabi -Sabi and Ichi -Go Ichi -E represent two key states.

The ikigai aims to make people think that true happiness does not lie in the final result but in doing.

Philosophy suggests focusing on small daily rituals while constantly maintaining a positive attitude.

Finding ikigai is not easy, Japanese culture teaches that a fundamental role is played by meditation.

Being able to find a purpose in life brings numerous advantages, tangible advantages to be able to face the everyday difficulties in a different way.

The ikigai allows you to:

1. enjoy the present
2. keep a focused mind
3. do not be overwhelmed by worries
4. feeling in control of oneself
5. One of the advantages deriving from ikigai is to enjoy a longer life expectancy

The Japanese are the longest-lived people in the world. This is due both to the healthy and balanced diet but also to the culture: the sense of community and living in harmony with oneself and with nature.

The Japanese have a culture distant from the Western one, too often focused on frenetic rhythms and a continuous search for maximum productivity.

The sense of life of the Japanese people is different, people:

- smile much more than Westerners
- they have learned to enjoy every moment of life
- they dedicate themselves to singing, dancing and music
- they have a real passion for what they do
- they help each other
- pursue activities that can relax them

- they keep the body and soul in balance

The secret of a long life, always reside precisely in the aforementioned points.

Finding a sense of one's life can appear to be an inflated phrase, belonging to distant cultures that then in fact no one is able to apply.

Finding your ikigai while remaining on the subject of advantages, so far it may seem like a Japanese philosophy that certainly has theoretical positive implications, but what do they translate into?

It is science, studies and research that demonstrate how much ikigai can impact on people's wellbeing.

Reduces anxiety

A study published in the Global Journal of Health Science shows that the prefrontal lobe of humans is more evolved than that of all other mammals. This leads to an innate need in people to spend their life meaningfully.

Pursuing the Japanese philosophy of ikigai means understanding the functioning of some traits of human behavior: ambition and emotions in general.

Knowing how to regulate one's emotions leads to a reduction in anxiety and a stimulation of pleasure and a sense of well-being.

It's good for the heart

As reported in a study featured in NIH: "The Meaning of Life Worth Living and Mortality in Japan", mortality risk and psychological factors are linked.

The study sampled 43,391 Japanese adults and asked them if they feel they have ikigai in their life.

The results showed that not pursuing this philosophy of life increases the risk of mortality due to cardiovascular disease or external causes.

However, no correlation has been found with cancer and there is no evidence that negative thoughts can increase the risk of mortality.

Increase self-confidence

Another research from the University of Virginia highlights how practicing ikigai allows people to increase self-confidence.

Japanese philosophy allows individuals to develop a whole series of internal values useful for making decisions independently without these being influenced by what society requires.

Knowing how to make decisions without being influenced by our surroundings can be useful, for example in correctly evaluating a job offer.

How can you not be influenced? According to the research, it is necessary to: learn to trust what your inner voice suggests, build a personal basis that can guide you in making decisions and prevent external events from controlling your decisions.

In other words, their internal values must guide the decision-making process.

Increase resilience

For example, the philosophy of life has helped many Japanese to overcome the emotional state caused by the earthquake that occurred in Japan in March 2011.

Live longer

As already pointed out, ikigai helps you live longer. As pointed out in a research by NHI given a population sample consisting of 30,155 men and 43,117 women, analyzed over the years, the results collected suggested that ikigai it is one of the factors that allows longevity to the Japanese people.

The changes, the state of uncertainty, a little or no definite future.

The covid 2019 is putting a lot of workers to the test. A new reality has now pervaded everyday life and the way of understanding work.

Ikigai could represent a philosophy to be adopted, useful for adapting quickly to changes, thus managing not to be crushed by anxiety, doubts and the thought of an uncertain future.

The rediscovery of the concept of ikigai could facilitate the construction of a purposeful life, aimed at enhancing one's skills and passions.

In a certain sense, ikigai applied to the world of work can be understood as an evolution of the concepts of social entrepreneurship.

That is, to imagine the birth of companies in the future that increasingly know how to enhance the talent of the worker on the one hand and respond to the needs of the world on the other.

It is therefore a question of achieving a balance. The entrepreneur or self-employed person can immediately try to direct their professional choices towards what really stimulates their creativity and passions.

Companies could delve into the concept of ikigai by trying to change certain aspects in the world in which they intend to work and value their staff.

For a company or for a self-employed worker being able to enhance what are the: interests, skills, knowledge and motivations can have the advantage of increasing competitiveness, productivity.

By generalizing and summarizing, finding a purpose in life cannot ignore finding a satisfying dimension within one's work sphere.

For this reason, a worker or an aspiring worker can use ikigai by defining:

What you are really good at

To achieve this, it may be useful to make a list of the results achieved and the positive feedback received. By doing this, you have a list of skills on which to start working and reflecting.

Past experiences

The past can tell a lot about which are the moments of work that have made the worker feel good. When you have felt particularly good or bad, they are experiences that are hard to forget. Bringing them back helps in defining ikigai .

What others think

Asking relatives, friends and colleagues for an opinion about yourself is another effective way to be able to define purpose and passions.

Finally, it is important to be aware that goals in life can change. It is not certain that what motivates a person today can motivate tomorrow in the same way. Ikigai is a journey of continuous self-discovery.

How to find the meaning of life

Japanese culture, as we have seen, suggests ikigai as a philosophy of life to be adopted. The advantages are innumerable and can be summed up with the phrase: do what you love and you will live a long time.

The philosophy is very interesting and supported by numerous research and case studies .

The Japanese should, therefore, really be a source of inspiration. A lot can be learned from this people.

In particular, in the community of Okinawa Island also known as: the place of longevity, the inhabitants adopting the ikigai and the results prove them right.

The friendly Japanese village is home to 3,000 people. They spend a life away from the hustle and bustle, close to the ocean, in harmony with nature and with themselves.

The population is happy, they cultivate their own vegetable garden and it is not uncommon to meet an ultra centenarian.

Okinawans also have very low rates of chronic disease and dementia rates are well below the global average.

As a result, ikigai is increasingly a point of reference for many people around the world.

Ikigai , therefore, as a philosophy of life whose concept and meaning can be defined in many ways. For some scholars ikigai starts from answering the questions at the beginning of the chapter, for others, one is enough: why do you get up in the morning?

Or, as psychiatrist and neurologist Viktor Frankl argues , the question may be: why don't you commit suicide? Or according to Dr. Sanjay Gupta another question could be: if there was no money so would you do in your life?

Unlike Ken Mogi, a famous Japanese neuroscientist and also the author of numerous texts on the subject, defines and equates the definition of ikigai with the famous slogan promoted during the Second World War by the British government : " Keep Calm and Carry on ".

Returning to Frankl , he used the fundamentals of ikigai to help his patients find their purpose in life. According to the psychiatrist, the feeling of emptiness and anxiety is due to an existential crisis.

He used, therefore, during therapy to guide patients towards the search for ikigai , defined as an essential fuel for living longer and happier.

Ultimately, there is no single question and there is no single path to take in order to find your ikigai . This can lie in the passion for cooking, writing, art, social relations and so on.

According to many inhabitants Ogimi shares in Japan ikigai resides in the cultivation of plants and vegetables, in others in the working with wicker.

Ikigai is a Japanese philosophy, following it helps you find your life purpose.

Once you find your ikigai as the Japanese teach, many ways of thinking decay, such as the idea that at a certain point in your life you have to retire or retire.

The secret seems to reside right here, in attributing importance to the right things, those that really allow us to feel good and that inevitably will accompany us throughout our life. It follows that the Japanese do not have a translation of the term "withdraw".

It is clear that behind a concept, there is a long way and hard work to be done. Modern life, the frenetic pace does not help. Money, power and success risk taking us away from ikigai .

To continue pursuing it without getting distracted, we report Mogi's advice.

He claims to follow five cornerstones: focus on the details, accept yourself as you are, rely on others, enjoy the present as an important moment.

The island of Okinawa, Japan, is known around the world for the longevity of its inhabitants. The opinion of various doctors is that diet, environment, genetics and lifestyle have found a practically perfect balance here: a secret recipe which also includes Ikigai , an exquisitely Japanese concept that we could translate as "the reason why wake up in the morning ".

In short, the meeting point between passion, mission, vocation and profession. "Your Ikigai is the intersection between what you are good at and what you love to do - explains Hector Garcia, one of the authors of the book" The Ikigai Method . The secrets of Japanese philosophy for a long and happy life ", published by Rizzoli. - Just as many people have always pursued fame and wealth, others have preferred to focus on something greater than their own material well-being. And this is precisely the point" .

So how to find our Ikigai ? The starting point would be a general basic curiosity, to which you can combine a series of four seemingly simple questions: "What do I love?", "What am I good at?", "What can I get paid for?" and "What does my reality need?". Four question marks that could easily fit into a university orientation questionnaire, in short, but which apparently would be the basis for a greater knowledge of oneself. And a happier life.

We give ten rules that would help to adopt the philosophy of the Okinawans are also listed. And to apply it successfully to your life, to stay healthy longer: let's run them together, then, and good Ikigai

.

Stay active and don't withdraw.

Give up stress and adopt a more bland lifestyle.

Only eat until you feel 80% full.

Surround yourself with good friends.

Stay fit and train every day.

Smile and be interested in the people around you.

Reconnect with nature.

Give thanks for what makes your life more beautiful and makes you feel alive.

Enjoy the moment.

Follow your Ikigai .

Printed in Great Britain
by Amazon

14891589R00092